MARKETING AND ECONOMICS

MARKETING AND ECONOMICS

by

MERLIN STONE
(Senior Lecturer, School of Management Education, Kingston
Polytechnic)

St. Martin's Press   New York

ISBN 0-312-51527-8

Library of Congress Cataloging in Publication Data

Stone, Merlin
  Marketing and economics.

  Includes bibliographical references and index.
  1. Marketing. 2. Economics. I. Title.
HF5415.S859   658.8   79-22206
ISBN 0-312-51527-8

To Ofra and Maya

Contents

1 Marketing and Economics – the Connection

This book attempts to relate the two disciplines of marketing and economics. Marketing is a task-oriented discipline. The task of the marketing manager is to structure the relations between his firm and its customers so as to further the achievement of the firm's business aims. Marketing, as a subject of study, aims to improve the marketing manager's efficiency in doing this job. Economics, although often used in a task-oriented way, is not defined in such a way. Economics is the study of the satisfaction of wants through the use of scarce resources. It analyses the processes and consequences of this want-satisfaction in a scientific manner.

The connection between the two disciplines lies in the fact that marketing exists because resources are scarce. The marketing manager works at the point where scarce resources and human wants meet. It is his task to 'manipulate' the scarce resources so as to satisfy human wants in a way that leads to the realisation of his firm's aims. He is therefore one of the key inhabitants of the world of wants and scarce resources that the economist claims to be in his domain.

This book aims to help the marketing practitioner exploit the teachings of economics. It is arranged according to the main analytical tasks and policy problems with which he has to deal. Marketing examples are used to illustrate these problems. Key points arising in economics that are of relevance to the marketer are discussed, while those points that will only impair understanding are set aside.

Given the recent academic history of marketing and economics, it could be argued that a dividing line between the two no longer exists. But although many articles that appear in economics journals would not be out of place in marketing journals (and vice versa), the difference in emphasis remains. However, this book does not try to divide the two subjects and does not hesitate to draw from the marketing literature that deals with the more 'economic' aspects of the subject.

In order to orientate the reader, let us first briefly consider what parts of economics should in principle be of use in marketing analysis. Many of the more useful concepts and results come from microeconomics. The principles of demand theory can make an important contribution to marketing analysis. The theoretical side of economics hypothesises about how buyers choose – from basic product choice theories to more complex ones on choice determined by characteristics in the product itself. The empirical side offers relevant work on the interpretation of statistical demand analyses and on the importance of particular variables in specific situations.

The theory of the firm deals with the way in which the resources of firms are applied to different activities, according to the aims of those owning or managing the business. This includes the determination of output levels at different price levels and under different demand conditions, levels of promotion and sales force activity and methods of distribution for that output. The theory provides us with useful concepts for describing and analysing different kinds of market behaviour and for investigating the consequences of different business aims in different competitive situations.

The origin of industrial economics as a subject lies principally in studies of the industrial structure of economies. A major data source for industrial economics is industrial classification statistics, which permit analysis of industrial production by industry groups and sub-groups. Although for marketing purposes there are sometimes problems caused by the non-coincidence of industrial classifications with markets, this data, when analysed by the statistical and analytical techniques of economics, is helpful in market structure and trend studies. The concentration of output in a few firms in an industry has implications for business policy because of the connection between industrial concentration and market structure. Similar studies (for example, of the relationship between concentration and profitability, concentration and stability of industrial structure and concentration and research and development intensity) can give more specific guidance for business policy. A particularly useful concept in this sort of analysis is that of 'barriers to entry' to new competition, which may be created by a variety of factors, including advertising, pricing policy, economies of scale, patents or high R and D spending. In framing marketing policy, account must be taken of how particular policies may produce changes in the structure of competition by changing the barriers to entry. In some countries, entry by import competition may be important, in which case a knowledge of international economics is useful.

The economics of innovation is also a field relevant to the study of the above topics. In this area (where social science and management disciplines are fairly well integrated), relevant topics include the rate of return to R and D expenditure, the relationship between innovation and industrial structure and the factors that determine the success and failure of innovations. All these factors are of some relevance for the analysis of product strategy.

The tools of economic analysis of production and cost are also useful for the analysis of costs of different marketing policies. Basic concepts, such as opportunity cost, can improve understanding of the cost information on which marketing decisions are based. The analysis of economies of scale is relevant to marketing decisions involving major changes in the level of the firm's activities.

The conventional distinction between microeconomics (which deals with individual decision making units – firms, consumers, investors, etc.) and macroeconomics (which deals with the behaviour of all decision makers of a certain class at the aggregate level) may not always help analysis. Some firms are so large relative to the economy in which they operate as to have a significant impact on the values of aggregate variables, such as output and investment. In such firms, business planners can be expected to take into account not only aggregate economic forecasts but also the impact of their own decisions on the macroeconomy. Macroeconomic analysis is based on the assumption that firms are small relative to the economy. It is important for the marketing practitioner to realise that much of the basic input into his market forecasts is based on macroeconomic methodology which may make questionable assumptions about the structure of relationships in the economy.

National income analysis is an important fact of macroeconomics because income forecasts underpin most market demand forecasts. Investment demand may also be a key indicator of likely developments in the economy, so marketing practitioners need to be able to assess its importance. The marketer needs also to be aware of monetary aspects, in particular the effect of inflation on real demand and on the appropriateness of particular methods of pricing and costing.

Another way of analysing the workings of the economy is through the use of input–output analysis. This is based on the notion that industries trade with each other in quantities determined by technical coefficients which relate their inputs to their outputs. Although there are certain theoretical and empirical problems associated with the use of this technique, it may provide a good basis for forecasting demand for the different industrial sectors.

The increasing importance of international trade and international monetary flows relative to domestic flows has had an important influence on the markets of many companies. This is so whether the company is directly involved in international activities, faces import competition or finds its costs affected by changes in the international economy. In certain areas of marketing analysis (particularly the more strategic ones), an understanding of some aspects of the working of the international economy is helpful. Relative prices in different economies are affected not only by movements in domestic costs and productivity but also by exchange rate changes and changes in government policies on international trade (import duties, quotas, export subsidies or levies, export financing and so on). These factors have important implications for the ease of entry into foreign markets and for the strength of import competition. At a more basic level, planning long-run marketing strategy may require knowledge of why it is that certain industries locate in some countries and not in others.

APPROACHING MARKETING ANALYSIS

We have seen that there are topics in economics that are relevant to marketing. The next step is to consider *how* economic theory can contribute to marketing analysis. To do this we begin in chapter 2 with an economic analysis of the aims and strategy of the company. The analysis helps to show where economics can make its contribution, and concludes that economics can help both through the analysis of how decisions are made and through the provision of methods for obtaining the information required to make those decisions. Chapter 3 therefore considers decision analysis, while aspects of information are considered in Chapters 4 to 7. Chapters 8 to 12 are concerned with the application of the methods of analysis described in the first half of the book to particular marketing policy areas.

2 Aims, Goals and Strategies

Marketing practitioners may find their work made more difficult by the fact that firms often have conflicting aims or goals and in the attempt to reach those goals, strategies which cut across each other are often employed. Consider the following simple example.

The export marketing manager of a small manufacturer of air conditioning products has embarked upon a sales drive in temperate climate countries. The market suddenly opens up because of a prolonged heat wave in some of these countries. The firm and its sales agents soon find themselves out of stock. The manager feels that his biggest chance of penetrating into these markets has been missed. He considers that the financial manager was wrong to cause stockbuilding to be restricted by persuading the managing director that the firm could not afford the required outlay. He feels that the firm's long-term profit aims and market diversification goals have been prejudiced by policies aimed at satisfying short-term cost minimisation and risk avoidance goals.

The marketing manager often finds himself in frustrating positions such as this because he is responsible for a task where two of the most basic and common general goals come into conflict, namely, satisfying the customer by providing a wide enough range of products when the customer wants them and at prices he can afford, and making profit by keeping revenue up and costs down. There is *a priori* no way of resolving this conflict, for the origin of the conflict lies in the basic economic problem of scarce resources. However, if the marketing manager fully understands the framework of aims, goals and strategies within which he works and which he helps to set up, then the chances are that he will be able to do his job better. Economics can help the marketer in coming to a better understanding of this framework and in working within it by analysing the logical relationship among aims, goals and strategies and by helping in assessments of the feasibility of different aims etc. But first of all we need to define clearly the terms aims, goals and strategies.

AIMS, GOALS AND STRATEGIES

We define these terms, using a sporting analogy, in the following way. The *aim* of a firm is the most general justification for any policy (parallel to winning the game). A *goal* is the justification for some policies but not necessarily for all policies (parallel to attempts to score goals or points, make runs and so on). A *strategy* is the general means adopted in attempts to reach goals (parallel to playing an attacking or offensive game, dominating particular parts of the ground, etc.). At the most specific level come *policies*, which are the ways in which particular strategies are implemented. We use the term *target* to cover all four terms. A brief example will make these definitions clear.

Suppose that the chief executive of a company, after consultation with his board, decides that the company should be aiming at a pre-tax rate of return on capital of 15 per cent and a real sales growth of 10 per cent. This is the *aim* of the firm. In order to reach these targets, the chief executive fixes a series of *goals* for his managers in consultation with them. For his marketing manager he fixes sales targets for particular product groups subject to restrictions on the price reduction and on costs incurred in making sales. For his production manager he sets a cost reduction goal subject to the achievement of particular production goals. (Note that goals are not necessarily the targets of functional managers.) Working on this basis, the marketing manager decides on his future strategies. He may decide that in one market he wants to take an innovative approach, launching a range of new products, while in others he wants to take an imitative strategy, maintaining his position with a pricing policy backed by good distributor account service. He may decide that competition is too intense in some markets and that the company should diversify out of them.

THE FIXING OF TARGETS[1]

A firm's business targets depend upon the personal aims and motivations of those who own or run the firm, as limited by its competitive situation. In a situation of intense competition, the firm that is committed to survival may have little option as to the targets that it adopts. If all the other firms against whom it is competing strive for maximum profits, and if there are no restrictions on the availability of inputs, the form of competition, etc., the firm may be forced to go for maximum profits in order to survive. In practice, competition rarely forces firms out of business if they are only slightly less efficient than their competitors. Competition of such intensity would require all firms to have complete information on market opportunities and production technologies. In most markets, competing firms have different information on the market opportunities available, would exploit those opportunities in different ways, are able to protect their own markets, and so on. This lack of tightness in the competitive framework allows other factors to influence the firm's targets. In a given competitive area, firms can survive for long periods with fundamentally different attitudes to targets.

The process of fixing targets of different degrees of generality is an iterative process, which requires referring back and forth to check consistency and feasibility. To start this process, managers and owners need to decide on the business aims of the firm. These can then be checked in the light of the goals and strategies that need to be feasible if the overall aim is to be reached. General aims which seem feasible may be set, but when the goals to achieve these aims are set, it may turn out that there are no feasible strategies which enable these goals to be reached. This may imply some revisions in the firm's aims.

OWNERSHIP, MANAGEMENT, ORGANISATION AND TARGETS

Whether a large number of shareholders, owner-managers, the government or some other public body, the owners are in principle the initiators of the business. They can decide to close it down, to change its structure, and so on. In a purely private enterprise firm, the interests of the owners will normally be profit-related. They may not want to maximise current profit, for they may be interested more in the long-term growth of assets. They may be interested more in a stable rate of growth of net worth than a fluctuating one with a higher expected value over the long term.

The management of firms which are publicly or communally owned may not be directly responsible to owners but responsible instead to their representatives.[2] In such firms, the main aim of the owners, as seen by their representatives, may be a maximum level of service subject to some budgetary constraint.

In some firms, ownership and management are one and the same, so there is no possibility of conflict between the aims of owners and those of managers. In many firms, the separation of ownership and management affects the adoption and pursuit of targets.[3] Managers have their own reasons for working, including the need to earn a living, the need for status, interest, job-satisfaction, and so on. These needs influence the decisions managers make. If cash flow permits, staff who are not strictly needed may be taken on or machines that are not necessary may be ordered because they increase the status or interest of a manager's job. Status, success, etc. may be judged by criteria which are not directly related to company aims. Risk avoidance may appear because even slight policy failures are paid for personally, even though the optimum strategy for the company might be to go for high risk, high return policies.

Management decisions are often made jointly. Decisions can be seen as the outcome of the formation of coalitions between the parties involved in the business.[4] Policy coalitions may be maintained at the expense of 'side payments' to members of the coalition. These payments may be of a monetary (for example, wages to workers, dividends to stockholders) or policy (concessions to managers responsible for other policy areas) nature. This bargaining nature of policy formulation may also apply to target formulation. Bargaining may take place among marketing, production and finance managers over production and stockbuilding targets for the coming year. This may concern the implications of production and stockbuilding targets for success in each manager's own policy area, his work load, and so on. Compromises will be made, involving concessions and trade-offs, until an acceptable policy combination is reached.

Much of the conflict in organisations is not resolved by removal of the source of conflict but patched up by temporary solutions, so the conflict tends to reappear. Inconsistencies among aims, goals and strategies may never be resolved and therefore be a source of recurring conflict, especially if particular managers become associated with particular targets. There is also a tendency to avoid dealing with uncertainty by concentrating on short-run aspects and by employing rules for decision making which emphasise short-run reactions to short-run feedback. This applies particularly to target formulation, for it is difficult to formulate targets in the light of developments which *might* occur in the long term. This same 'limiting' tendency appears in problem-solving behaviour, where the search for solutions may be closely confined to the problem area and to current alternatives. Similarly, solutions tend to be accepted because of feasibility rather than because of demonstrated superiority to other solutions. Targets are therefore likely to be adopted after a relatively limited search process. In setting and analysing targets, therefore, managers need to be aware of their tendency to avoid dealing with the long term, to accept targets because of similarity to existing ones, to be content with the most feasible rather than with the best of a set of alternatives, and to adopt targets which only temporarily patch up conflicts.

AIMS OF THE FIRM

The kinds of aims adopted by firms include target rate of return on capital, target rate of increase of sales, target rate of growth of net assets, maintenance of overall market share and maintenance of employment levels. Such aims may be combined with qualifying aims, such as risk avoidance, involvement in particular kinds of markets, and so on. The aims will normally be expressed for present and future periods, and may be combined with other aims of the same degree of generality (e.g. profit and sales aims). In such cases, the degree of trade-off between aims needs to be clearly established before policy can flow effectively from aims.[5] Multiplicity of aims may increase the complexity of the management process at every level, so it is worth considering each aim to see whether it could be amalgamated with some other aim.

AIMS

Aims, goals and strategies are set not in isolation but with reference to the environment and capabilities of the firm. Targets need to be checked for feasibility. This does not imply a minimalist policy of accepting only those targets known definitely to be feasible, but rather that effort should not be wasted on trying to achieve targets which are not feasible if that effort may reduce performance below levels that would have been achieved if targets had been more realistic. The crucial ingredient in the judgement of feasibility is information. Without information on the possibilities open to the firm and on the real use value of the resources available to the firm, errors may be made in the establishment of targets. At the lowest level of targets, those associated with particular marketing policies, identification of the kinds of information required may not be too difficult. For example, the information required to assess the feasibility of a particular pricing policy for a given product is about demand for the product, cost conditions and competitors operating in the same area. The kind of information needed to assess the feasibility of overall business aims is much more general. Making reliable assessments of its implications for business aims is much more difficult. Let us consider an example.

Industrial Components, Inc. (IC) is a manufacturer of clutches, transmissions and couplings for various kinds of factory machines. In the previous few years it has made a return on capital (net of tax but gross of depreciation) of 10 per cent, while inflation has been running at about 4 per cent. Its market valuation has been falling and the Board is worried about the possibility of a take-over attempt from either of the firm's two main competitors, both of whom have been making rates of return on capital (on the above basis) of between 15 and 20 per cent in the same period. Market shares of the major firms over the previous few years have been approximately as follows:

AB Clutches and Couplings, Inc.	35 %
JK Transmissions, Inc.	25 %
Industrial Components, Inc.	20 %
Williams Power, Inc.	10 %
Others	5 %
Imports	5 %

The market is fairly competitive on prices, but each manufacturer has some patented designs which enable him to charge higher prices for certain products. Importers normally sell at prices which are about 10 per cent less, but find it difficult to compete because of the importance of parts distribution and servicing.

IC has spent about 5 per cent of its turnover on development in the past five years; this is thought to be a substantially higher proportion than the other firms. As a result IC has a number of new products in the pipeline for which patent applications have been filed. Given all these factors, IC's top management is trying to decide what would be a realistic target profit rate for the coming years, taking into account the pressing need to increase profitability.

Instead of simply choosing as a target a profit figure equal to that of one of the major competitors, the company president decides that some fundamental analysis is necessary before a target profit figure can be fixed. The first stage of the process is to decide what information would be necessary in principle to reach a decision. He sets up a working group to establish what information is required.

The working group's report divides the information required into three groups: demand information, competitor information and internal information. The division is justified as follows:

If the company is to adopt a feasible profits target, then it needs to examine what market opportunities are possible. This means examining the present and likely future state of demand for existing products, demand for new products, customer needs for services supplied with products, and so forth. We then need to analyse what competitors are likely to be doing, how the marketing strategy for their existing products is likely to develop, where they are likely to concentrate their new product development and product improvements, and so on. The possibility of changes in the competitive structure of the industry (for example through take-overs, entry of new competition) must be taken into account. The company itself needs to be subjected to thorough scrutiny, including the possibility of cost reductions through the rationalisation of product lines and production, distribution and stocks. The company's market and product development strategy needs to be re-examined, in order to establish the effectiveness of past policies. The question of whether the company has been organised for profitability also needs to be examined.

The working group then produced the following listing of factors relevant to the fixing of the profits aim.

Demand

1. Level of aggregate investment in plant and equipment in the economy over the next few years (major determinant of new – as opposed to replacement – demand for the products);

2. level of aggregate economic activity over the next few years (determinant of the above factor and of the level of replacement demand; this is because increased output by customer firms leads to increased wear and tear depreciation and increased funds for replacing equipment);

3. increase in demand likely as a result of general substitution for labour of equipment employing our components;

4. likely increase in sales as a result of launching the new products, less any decrease due to erosion from competitive products, taking into account likely changes in competitors' policies;

5. export market opportunities.

The following rider accompanied this listing:

> These are the main items on which we need information. If no satisfactory independent information is obtainable for a particular item, then we shall also need information on the determinants of that item in order to build our own model for predicting it. The factors can be divided into three groups: (i) long-term structural factors (e.g. substitution of capital equipment for labour); (ii) economic contingencies (evolution of overall demand and of investment expenditure by firms over the next few years); and (iii) factors related to our particular market.

Competition
1. Analysis of profitability figures over the past few years;
2. analysis of cost structure over past few years, in particular costs of individual products and funds allocated to development and marketing;
3. organisation of development, production and marketing;
4. likely developments in marketing policy;
5. key potential entrants, chances of entry, implications for market structure;
6. future impact of imports, assessment of chances of increased or reduced penetration, chances of major relative price changes (for example as a result of exchange rate changes).

The working group commented that the aim of this analysis should be to establish what has led to competitors' higher profitability in the past and what they are likely to do in the future which will affect IC's market position and profitability.

Internal factors
1. Current cost conditions for all IC's products; likely improvements in cost conditions as a result of changes in production techniques, learning, more efficient buying, substitution of cheaper materials, more efficient stock-building policy, economies of scale, and so on;
3. reduction in price made possible by reduction of research and development effort (or any other overhead);
4. extent to which higher prices can be obtained for new products, increased sales from marketing policy changes.

The working group commented that information was needed on all possible ways of increasing revenue relative to costs; the above listing covered the factors considered to be of the greatest potential for IC.

The above example demonstrates the breadth of the information needed to judge the feasibility of a particular business aim. The lists are not comprehensive, reflecting as they do the working group's prior assessment of the most important areas for investigation.

GOALS

The information required to assess goal feasibility is more specific than in the case of aims. In IC's case, review of the various possibilities open to the firm may lead to the conditional conclusion that a 15 per cent rate of return on capital is feasible on the condition that certain goals are feasible. In the marketing area, one of the goals may be an increase in market share to 25 per cent over three years, given that the profit margin on sales can be maintained. The information required to assess the feasibility of this goal would be specifically concerned with competitive reaction to IC's strategies for achieving this goal and with the cost implications of expanding output and product range.

STRATEGIES

The feasibility of goals is conditional on the feasibility of the strategies that might be adopted to achieve the goals. Here information needs will be even more specific. For example, one strategy that IC might use to reach their market share goal is to use the new products to penetrate those parts of the market which were formerly the exclusive preserve of its two major competitors. The information required here will include performance comparisons of products, servicing characteristics of products, requirements of customers who bought solely from the two majors (their purchasing procedures, organisational characteristics, and so on) as well as more general information concerning probable competitors' reaction to such a move.

In the light of the above, it should be stressed that marketing managers must keep rethinking their own goals and strategies, to question the feasibility of these targets and of their firm's overall business aims. To be able to do this, managers need to have the appropriate information inputs.

ECONOMIC GUIDELINES TO TARGET FEASIBILITY

Although no target can *a priori* be said to be feasible, targets can be subjected to economic analysis to establish some of the conditions for feasibility. Here, we take one example from each level of target, as follows:

Aims: rate of return on capital
Goals: market share for one product
Strategies: first into the market with new products

RATE OF RETURN ON CAPITAL AIM

In its most general sense, the rate of return on capital refers to the relationship between net revenue (sales revenue less costs – including depreciation – but before deduction of profits taxation or non-profit payments to capital, that is to pay interest) and capital (of all kinds) employed. A more restrictive interpretation is to take the rate of return on risk capital (that part of capital excluding bonds, bank credit, etc.). The former measure is probably a better measure of commercial success, because it is unaffected by success or failure in financial strategy. There are three basic economic theories on the origin of profit: compensatory and functional theories, frictional and monopoly theories and technology and innovation theories.

Compensatory and functional theories One function of profit is to compensate the entrepreneur or group entrepreneurship for the use of their talents, contacts and so on. The more talented the management team, the more profits they can make by exploiting commercial opportunities. Some firms require relatively little capital, but substantial inputs of 'business know-how', contacts, and so on. This may be reflected in very high rates of return on capital. This suggests that one way of raising the firm's rate of return on capital is by exploiting managerial resources more effectively in ways that do not require large injections of capital. In the long term, profitability may be increased by investing in managerial resources.

Profit also compensates investors for giving up their use of capital and for accepting risk. Capital is required because of the 'round-aboutness' of production (meaning the time it takes for an expenditure on inputs to be recouped by sales revenue). Holding of stocks of inputs or finished goods, purchasing of machines and investment in research and development are among the major contributors to round-aboutness. A firm's relative unprofitability may sometimes be traceable to too much round-aboutness, whether in the form of too high stock levels, expenditure on unnecessary equipment (or expenditure too early), too much investment in research which turns out to have no immediate commercial application or too long a delay before accounts are paid. For this reason, it may pay to analyse certain basic business ratios (for example proportion of turnover held as stock, average accounts outstanding, research–turnover ratio) when considering the feasibility of increasing profits.

Generally speaking, riskier investments would not be undertaken if higher profits were not expected from them. Given the choice between a certain rate of return and a risky investment with the same expected rate of return, most investors will choose the risk-free investment. One way in which a firm can increase its rate of return on capital is to take more risks, not in the trivial sense of being less careful, but in the sense of picking out areas where the expected value of gains is higher but where there is less certainty about the outcome. Whether a firm can profit from this depends on whether investors are able to assess the risks of the firm's policies more efficiently than the firm itself. It also depends on whether the firm's competitors have taken up most such opportunities and whether the firm itself can absorb increased riskiness (which may depend on size, financial resources, etc.). Note too that the ability to manage in risky situations is a management resource which commands its own price.

Frictional and monopoly theories of profit A frictional factor is technically one which prevents equilibrium being restored immediately, once that equilibrium has been disturbed. Frictional factors affect the rate at which new technologies are exploited and the speed with which new buyer demands are met, irrespective of the state of competition in a particular industry. Even if the resources to exploit a change are available, it takes time for a firm to organise itself to use the resources. If the *structure* of competition prevents, say, the marketing of products by particular firms in order to satisfy a particular demand, then monopoly factors may be at work.

Frictional and monopolistic profits can be created by any barrier to entry; examples include buyer preferences for existing products or brands, locational advantages, cost advantages stemming from economies of scale, possession of specialist knowledge, patents, control over inputs or outlets, international trade barriers, cartel arrangements, and so on.[6] In assessing the feasibility of particular profit aims, firms need to take into account the extent to which factors such as the above can be exploited by themselves or their competitors.

Technology and innovation theories of profit The application of new technologies or methods to product design, production or management can provide increased profit. Given that there are frictional and monopoly elements in the competitive framework which prevent rapid imitation of innovation, higher profits from innovation may last for some time, although they are likely to be eroded eventually by firms that imitate or overtake.[7] Ways of protecting these profits include erecting barriers to entry or adopting a policy of continuous innovation. The feasibility of making profits in this way depends on a firm's ability to improve its technology in ways that would cut production costs significantly (particularly in ways that are not easily imitated or overtaken), improve its products so that they can command larger markets and/or higher prices than those of competitors and making innovations in management methods.

Empirical evidence on rates of return Much of the empirical work that has been done in this area has concentrated on the effects of market structure. There is good evidence of a strong positive relationship between industrial concentration and profitability, although there are several views about the exact nature of the relationship.[8] The strength of the relationship varies among industries. There is also evidence of a relationship between the rate of growth of net assets and profitability (although here the causation may be in both directions), as well as between barriers to entry and profitability.[9] The implication for management is that achieving higher rates of return on capital is aided by barriers to entry, by being in a concentrated industry and (perhaps) by being a relatively fast-growing firm.

There is some evidence of an association between sustained R and D programmes or flows of innovation on the one hand and growth and profitability of firms on the other (although here too there are doubts about the direction and nature of causation).[10] High R and D expenditure in itself may create higher barriers to entry and hence higher profits. However, there is clearly an association between innovativeness and profitability. Note that this may partly be due to profits accruing as a return to accepting risk or to the application of R and D resources of a kind that are not easily obtainable.

MARKET SHARE GOAL FOR ONE PRODUCT

Market share goals emphasise sales performance in relation to that of competitors and are more likely to be employed where the market is dominated by a few firms. Expressing sales goals in market share terms normally results from having to consider competitive reaction to policies. In situations where competitors' policies depend upon the firm's own policies, difficulty in predicting competitors' reactions to the firm's policies may produce considerable uncertainty about the outcome of competitive situations. This may lead firms in oligopolistic situations to avoid frequent use of certain kinds of policy (e.g. pricing).[11] In assessing the feasibility of particular market share goals, it is important to identify which competitive weapons are useful means of increasing or maintaining market share. Let us consider some possibilities.

Price cuts The appropriateness of pricing as a way of increasing or maintaining market share depends on the degree of differentiation of the firm's product from its competitors' products. Where products are identical (that is to say perceived as such by consumers) and price information freely available and well diffused, reductions in price to increase market share are only advisable where:

a) the price elasticity of demand is greater than unity. It may be that the sensitivity of demand to price changes has been misjudged in the past. This often applies to segments of the market which firms have not previously considered analysing separately. The firms that are first to reach the conclusion that price cutting is appropriate may be able to make permanent gains. The elasticity of costs with respect to output and the availability of capacity for increased production need to be taken into account here.
b) there is a chance of forcing less efficient firms out of business. Here, the firm must check that its costs are in line with those of the most efficient firms in the market and that it has the capacity to take advantage of sales opportunities. Less efficient firms with substantial liquid assets may be able to survive a protracted price war in which for some time all firms are losers. In such situations, relatively efficient firms may be able to increase their market shares. Higher profits generated by greater efficiency can be used in investment to differentiate products, to increase distribution efficiency or to improve market information systems. However, if higher efficiency is generated by increased turnover, then price cuts may be justified.

In markets where products are differentiated, additional competitive weapons are available. Firms attempting to use price cuts to increase market share may find their competitors reacting with policies of increased promotion, further product differentiation, etc. Each type of policy is likely to have different effects over time. A firm may invest profit in price cutting with some success in the short run, but this may push competitors to invest in long-term ways of increasing or maintaining their market shares, once they realise their vulnerability to price cuts. If competitors are multi-product firms, they will be able to ride short-term problems caused by competitive price cuts more easily. Market share goals in differentiated product markets should be formulated by taking into account the variety of competitive weapons available other than price and the short and long-term implications of each of those weapons.

Other competitive weapons As there is a multiplicity of ways in which market share goals might be attained, assessing the feasibility of particular goals requires an analysis of a series of factors. These include the effect on the firm's business aims of the various policies that might be used to achieve the goal, the effect of each policy on the extent to which competing firms will achieve their business aims, the costs to competing firms of the policies they might be forced to adopt to defend their own market shares and the general way in which the long-run course of competitive developments is affected by the original policy change. To analyse these factors, management has to consider a number of possible scenarios, each consisting of a sequence of actions and reactions, ranging over all policy areas – price, promotion, distribution, product quality, etc. Let us extend the example of Industrial Components to demonstrate this.

Suppose that achieving the 15 per cent rate of return on capital is reckoned to be conditional on achieving the market share goal of 25 per cent within three years. The first scenario that marketing management investigates is that of putting the complete portfolio of new products on the market within a year. The firm's R and D effort has produced four new products, two of which attack the key markets of the market leader, AB, one of which attacks the main market of JK Transmissions, while the fourth is designed to compete with imports. Assuming that information about competitors' policies and buyer behaviour was available, the action reaction sequence might be depicted as in Figure 2.1, which illustrates only one 'branch' of this 'tree of possibilities'. We see that the assumption is that the products will be launched in the second quarter of Year 1. Assuming the likelihood of slow initial diffusion of the new product and the dependence of the short-term market on replacement demand (where customer loyalty is relatively strong), IC considers it necessary to make its technically superior products financially more attractive in the short term by extending the credit period by three months. In spite of IC's relatively weak profits position, this cash flow sacrifice is reckoned to be essential to overcome buyer resistance. Price cutting is considered to be too risky a strategy.

Market research may provide the firm with some of the information required to assess likely competitor reaction. Market segmentation and product positioning studies should enable IC to find out what marketing policy combinations are likely to be effective in countering these policies. Linking this kind of analysis with an analysis of the resources possessed by competitive firms may give some indication of the likelihood of particular competitors following different kinds of policies. It may be possible to evaluate the impact of such a 'policy tree' on company aims by working out the consequences of each action and counteraction for, say, profitability and attaching probabilities to each branch. Such an evaluation, however subjective, may help in assessing the extent to which achievement of business aims is dependent on the pursuit of the goal in question.

FIRST INTO MARKET WITH NEW PRODUCTS STRATEGY

The feasibility of such a strategy depends on several factors. One group of factors may be labelled *technological*. For example, if new product success in a particular industry typically involves the use of leading-edge technology in production or product design, then continuous success with this kind of strategy will require constant updating of the firm's production methods or products. In practice, there may be constant threats from other firms to outdate the firm's technology. The feasibility of the strategy will therefore depend on whether the firm can allocate enough resources to the process and whether it is organisationally capable of sustaining the effort required.

A second group of factors relate to *demand*. For example, if new products typically involve major departures in the dimensions of consumer demand that are satisfied, then the first product into the market may yield more information about the characteristics that buyers do *not* want embodied in the product. Even if first products judge the market accurately, they may have to carry most of the burden of

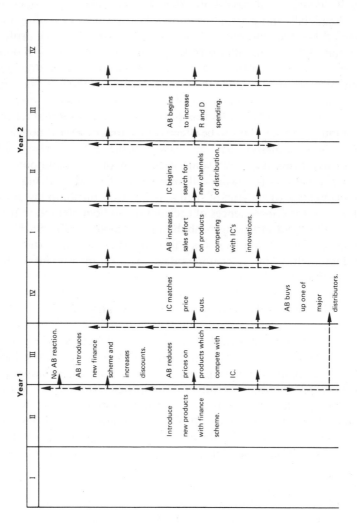

Fig. 2.1.

diffusion of a new concept, allowing later firms to exploit the work. Possibilities such as these need to be offset against the more obvious benefits of being first into the market (possibility of capturing the market and setting up barriers to entry, learning a new technology more quickly, taking advantage of economies of scale earlier on in the product's history, attracting key personnel, and so on).

The costs and benefits of being first into the new market are dependent on market structure. In oligopolistic situations, often characterised by high defensibility of competitive positions (once they have been established), being first into the market may be made difficult by intense competition by other firms to be first. Once the position is achieved, the pay-off is high.[12] Strength of sales network also affects the feasibility of such a strategy on a continuing basis. A firm with a weakly developed sales network may take so long to market its innovations that its competitors may come out with better products before the original firm has had the chance to profit from its product. This may prejudice its chances of innovating successfully the next time. Imitation may be a more appropriate strategy under certain conditions, particularly if it is rapid.[13] However, well-established firms with well-established products may have buyer loyalty working so strongly in their favour that they are able to take longer over development, reap the rewards of using competitors' experience with new technologies or new dimensions of buyer wants, and target their products more accurately (and profitably).

Schumpeter's theory of economic progress,[14] which sees the process of innovation as one of 'creative destruction' of old products and sometimes established firms, implies that the firm which initially succeeds by being first to the market is likely to be overtaken by other firms in this respect. This kind of process in production and process innovation is also implied by Downie.[15] He suggests that firms which have not innovated in the past are pressed by eroded markets and low profits to innovate to survive. This implies that firms will find it difficult to achieve sustained success by always being first to market, because of the pressure from other firms which need to get to the market first in order to survive. However, firms which originally succeeded by innovating may survive and retain profitability by erecting entry barriers. The suggestion that a particular strategy can give a firm a good chance of long-run success[16] should be set against evidence of continual changes in the relative performance of firms.[17] It might be more appropriate for firms to adopt a flexible approach to strategy as their competitive position and technology changes.

Case studies of firms that are innovators or imitators show various degrees of success accruing to each strategy.[18] The general point that arises from such studies is that the success of each strategy depends on competitive structure, which itself changes over time. This puts a premium on analysis designed to show the economic forces at work in competitive structures and how they affect the evolution of such structures.

TARGETS AND DECISIONS

We have considered some of the factors that affect the way in which targets are set and their feasibility. Target formulation is a complex process, affected by many factors: market structure, technology, organisational aspects of the firm, etc. Policies follow from these targets through decisions made by management on the basis of information about the firm and its environment. In Chapter 3 we consider some aspects of the way in which policy decisions are made, while in Chapters 4–6 we consider some of the economic information inputs into decisions.

3 Decision Analysis

Decision analysis examines the way in which decisions are made according to certain criteria and using particular information. In this chapter, we shall not describe in detail the various decision techniques that are used or have their roots in economics. For this we refer the reader to any text on managerial economics.[1] Rather, we concentrate on certain methodological issues involved in the analysis of marketing decisions.

A decision technique needs to have certain basic characteristics if it is to be useful in marketing decisions. These include

Data availability The data that the technique requires must be either obtainable (in the case of information about the past or the present) or able to be forecast (in the case of information about the future), at a cost which is justifiable by the improvement in marketing performance that the technique may make possible. This implies that some techniques may be feasible when they are used to analyse important decisions but not when they are used to analyse minor decisions.

Computational feasibility The computations that are required by the decision technique should be feasible and not cost more than is justifiable by the improvement in marketing performance that the technique may make possible. Computational feasibility depends on factors such as the kind of decision being taken, the complexity of the relationships between the variables involved and the number of variables. For example, it may be feasible to analyse a certain type of problem where there are twenty variables and constraints, with all the interrelationships linear, but not feasible when the number of variables and constraints is much larger and the interrelationships curvilinear.

As well as satisfying these general conditions, decision techniques need to be able to deal with a number of more specific points:

Continuity or discreteness of variables Marketing decisions may concern continuous variables, which can assume an infinity of possible values, or in practice close to infinity (variables such as price, stock levels and promotional budget) and discrete variables, which can take on only a limited set of values (such as the number of products to be marketed). Whether a technique can handle the continuity or discreteness of variables may depend on the way in which data are presented for analysis. For example, discrete variables may be incorporated into a continuous variable analysis by the use of dummy variables (see p. 83), while techniques designed for continuous variables may be transformed for discrete analysis by adding constraints which confine variables to, for example, integer values. In this way, linear programming can be transformed into integer programming to handle physical distribution and other assignment problems.

Type of target involved A decision technique needs to be able to accommodate the type of target involved. A target may involve not only maximising or minimising but also achieving a target level of performance. There may be constraints involved. The target may be composed of one or many variables. If maximisation of one variable is what is required, then calculus (marginal analysis) may be used if all the variables which are inputs into the analysis are continuous and the relationships known. More complex targets may be handled by constructing weighted target indices or by taking parts of the target as constraints. Even where the relationships are discontinuous and the targets composed of more than one variable, it should be possible to handle the problem using the various programming techniques used in operations research, so long as the trade-off between target variables is known. Trade-offs can be established by using conjoint or other multivariate analysis of past decisions to establish the weights to be attached to each target variable. Where constraints are elastic (meaning they may be violated, but only at a cost), the same approach can be used.

Risk and uncertainty Most information used in marketing decisions has an element of uncertainty attached to it. Whether this is the result of the statistical procedure used to estimate a relationship (see p. 80) or the result of a subjectively assigned probability (e.g. for estimating a competitor's reaction to a given marketing strategy), decision techniques need to be able to handle this. Most techniques work on the basis of particular values for variables rather than means and variances. Simulation exercises (repeated running through of the decision technique with values of the variables chosen either according to their distributions or, when the distribution is not known, at random within a specified range) can be used to derive the sensitivity of a particular decision to risk and uncertainty.

Interdependence between decisions A common characteristic of marketing decisions is that they affect other decision areas within the firm. For example, sales decisions affect production efficiency through batch size, stock holding, and so on. Because of the complexity of the interaction among decision areas, firms sometimes consider them separately, with policy in one area considered as a constraint in another. Decisions which are interdependent should ideally be taken jointly and the technique used adapted to take account of the likely multiplicity of targets, constraints and variables.

Time structure of decisions Decisions made today have lasting effects which may preclude decisions that might have been taken in the future. Multi-period analysis usually requires incorporating some discounting procedure to enable information about the present and the future to be treated on an equal basis. Because achieving a particular target today may affect the chances of achieving another target in the future, the trade-off between targets over time should normally be included in decision analysis.

Most economic decision analysis concerns maximisation or minimisation. Marginal analysis, which consists of working out the effects on the objective function (target) of small changes in decision variables, is used to isolate the conditions under which maximisation or minimisation takes place. In the case of profit maximisation, the general condition is that each variable which contributes to profit should be used until the extra revenue yielded as a result is just offset by the extra cost of using that variable (the principle of equating marginal cost and marginal revenue). As long as the relationship between the target and the variable is continuous, calculus may be used in decision making. Constraints can be handled in this analysis by using Lagrangian multipliers.[2] Although the marginal approach may be of limited usefulness in marketing decisions because of the nature of the data, the vocabulary of marginal analysis is useful in defining the many allocation problems the marketing manager has to deal with.

ALLOCATION PROBLEMS

Many marketing policy decisions concern the allocation of resources to different uses. For example, sales policy decisions may concern the allocation of output between markets of customers, the allocation of promotional budget between different promotional methods and the allocation of territories among salesmen. Product policy decisions involve the allocation of the firm's resources among its different products. The maximising solution to allocation problems is to allocate each resource to the market, product, etc., to which it makes the greatest contribution to achievement of the target, up to the point at which extra units of the resource would make a greater contribution to reaching the target by being allocated elsewhere, taking into account any interdependence in the effects of different resources.

Another way of looking at this solution is to say that each resource (unit of output, salesman, unit of advertising expenditure) has an *opportunity cost*, which is defined as the value to the firm of what is forgone by not being able to use the resource in the best alternative way. Thus the opportunity cost of a unit of output sold in one market is the highest price that could have been obtained for it in the best alternative market (assuming selling costs to remain constant). So the opportunity cost of a resource is not the money that has been paid to obtain it but the value of its best alternative use. If the outlay is greater than the value of the resource's best use and if the outlay can be returned or cancelled, then the resource's true opportunity cost is the outlay. In allocating resources among uses, the firm should be weighing returns against opportunity costs.

The use of these concepts makes substantial demands on a firm's information system, which has to provide information on the consequences of changes in the values of a wide range of variables, taking into account any interdependence in their effects. If the information system can meet these demands, then it should be possible to use some of the programming techniques currently applied in operations research.

For example, linear programming can handle the problem of maximising an objective function under conditions of discontinuous choice, although it imposes the limiting assumption of linearity of all the relationships (implying no economies of scale, no declining marginal revenues, etc.). Suppose that a marketing manager who wants to make as much profit as possible is making his product combination decision, but the resources he can use for producing and marketing the total product range are limited. Linear programming would handle this problem by taking one combination of products known to be feasible (given resource constraints and production functions), finding which resource reallocation among products increased profits most, and repeating the process until no resource reallocation increases profits.

Where relationships are non-linear, more complex programming methods have to be used, but the philosophy, if not the method, remains the same. A useful part of the data output of linear programming is a set of shadow prices which are the opportunity costs of each input. These can be compared with the outlays required to obtain the inputs to see if acquiring more of a particular input is justified.

If a firm's targets are not expressed in terms of maximisation, decision analysis becomes slightly more complicated. Satisficing (the adoption of target levels of performance such that performance *beyond* these levels is not particularly sought) does not provide management with a very firm guide to action. Consider the difference between the profit maximiser and the satisficer. The economic caricature of the profit maximiser is that of a manager hungry for limitless amounts of profit. He sees an opportunity for profit and seizes it, but makes sure that the move will not detract from his long-run net profits (as calculated on a discounted cash flow basis) and takes into account the true opportunity cost of every resource used in exploiting the opportunity (and hence the extent to which the opportunity precludes other more profitable opportunities). The satisficer, on the other hand, owes the fact that he is able to satisfice rather than maximise to the existence of a certain amount of slack in the competitive framework. This slack means that he does not have to take up every profitable opportunity. Profitable opportunities may be rejected because it is felt that there are easier or simpler ways of making the profits target. Decision analysis based on maximisation principles is one of a series of inputs which enters into the satisficer's calculations as to which combination of policies will enable him to reach his targets most easily, with most status to himself, with least risk, or according to any other of a whole range of possible decision criteria. Put another way, the satisficer usually has additional (implicit) targets to consider in making decisions. Once these targets are identified (note that they may be changing all the time while the basic satisficing target remains constant), then conventional decision analysis may be applicable, although there may be problems in quantifying the additional targets and establishing trade-off rates between them.

SEARCHING FOR INFORMATION AND SOLUTIONS

Marketing management normally spends a large part of the time which is allocated to policy decisions in searching for information and possible solutions. Management needs to obtain information about markets, product possibilities, costs, distributors, promotional methods and so on. Policy solutions have to be identified before they can be evaluated. Although it may be clear that a new product or a new promotional message is needed, merely establishing what *kind* of product or message can take up time and resources. Searching takes time and resources. A major problem of the profit maximiser is that of deciding how much of his resources to allocate to search, given that the productivity of past search may not be a good indicator of the productivity of future search.

Marketing management in satisficing firms do not face such a serious problems concerning search. Suppose that for the current year the firm is almost certain to achieve its targets. In such a situation, search activity does not cease, unless the firm is prepared to increase the risk that targets will not be reached in future years. Search activity, coupled with activity directed to reinforcing the firm's market and technical position, will continue. If search is reduced, it is because some other 'security-increasing' activity is being increased. In principle, one should be able to analyse decisions in such situations in terms of profit and sales *constraints* and certainty *maximising* (that is to say, risk minimising) for policies such as information search, market defence and technological defence (research and development activities).

ATTITUDES TO RISK AND UNCERTAINTY

We have indicated that risk and uncertainty can be handled in decision analysis by simulation aimed at showing the consequences of information-based risk for decision outcomes. However, the importance of risk and uncertainty in decision-making depends on the attitudes of decision makers to those decisions. These attitudes are likely to be quite volatile. A manager's willingness to accept the risky element of a policy depends partly on the current state of affairs in his firm – in particular in those areas of activity for which he is responsible. If a firm is well ahead of its profit target, managers may be more willing to accept riskier policies (on condition that their expected returns are higher than the returns from less risky policies). A recent failure in a manager's area of responsibility may cause him to assume a cautious attitude to risk.

There are various general classifications of attitudes to risk and uncertainty:

Expected value acceptance This describes willingness to accept expected value as certain. For example, if a manager has to choose between two sales agents for penetration into a new export market, and considers that one agent (A) has a chance of making a big success but also has a strong chance of not doing well, while the second agent (B) is almost certain to do reasonably well but unlikely to excel, then the choice might be set up as shown in Table 3.1

TABLE 3.1   Five-year sales (in $ thousand) (probabilities in parentheses)

	High	Medium	Low	EV
A	2000 (0.2)	1000 (0.3)	500 (0.5)	950
B	1500 (0.1)	1000 (0.7)	750 (0.2)	1000

In this situation, the expected value accepter would choose B. Reliable estimates of probabilities are unlikely to be obtainable, and the result is highly sensitive to probability estimates and to the particular sales levels that are chosen to represent the high, medium and low outcomes. However, it is usually worth making some attempt to set the situation up in this way to get some idea of the structure of the decision. In this case, the table might be based on the fact that A has very good contacts with the largest potential customers in the market but there is doubt about whether he will be able to exploit this position, while B has a good trading relationship with a large number of small potential customers.

Risk avoidance and acceptance Suppose that in the above example A had a 0.2 chance of making sales of $3m (instead of $2m). A risk avoider would choose B in spite of A's higher expected value because he would be worried about the relatively high chance of achieving only the low sales target of $0.5m. A risk accepter might pick A (even assuming the original figures) because of the chance of major success. A more balanced approach would be to consider the policy choice as part of a range of policy choices which together could comprise a risk portfolio. In this case, the firm behaves as a risk avoider in some policy choices and a risk accepter or expected value accepter in others. Such an approach needs to take into account the likely association between riskiness and profitability.

Managers sometimes see risk and uncertainty as phenomena they can influence, rather than as phenomena which are independent of them. As has been pointed out, risk and uncertainty can be reduced by obtaining more information or by following commercial or technological policies which increase the firm's control over its business environment.

Moreover, even if an adverse state of nature occurs, it may be possible to reduce its harmful consequences by hard work or (in the case of the firm which has a strong hold on its market) by investing heavily to attempt to maintain market position. For example, a product which seems likely to fail may be sustainable by increased marketing expenditure until a substitute can be found.

Surprise avoiders and accepters Shackle suggests that there is a central range of possible outcomes to each decision which would not cause any surprise if they occurred.[3] Within this range, outcomes can be dealt with by using the usual analysis. If there is a possibility of an outcome well outside this range, then it may dominate the decision, for the surprise avoider will tend to choose policies which are unlikely to produce unpleasant surprises.

Optimists and pessimists Managers are led by their nature and experience to be optimists or pessimists. This affects both their valuation of outcomes and their estimation of probabilities of particular outcomes.[4] There is room for optimism and pessimism both about the consequences of success and failure and about the chances of success and failure. Optimism will produce an upward bias in the returns and probabilities attached to successful outcomes and a downward bias in the adverse consequences and probabilities attached to unsuccessful outcomes. This tendency has an important influence on decision making in conditions of uncertainty.

Regret minimisers Savage suggests that one possible attitude to risk and uncertainty is formed by the desire to avoid regret.[5] Suppose that the marketing manager of a domestic appliance manufacturer has to decide how much stock to build for a given model in the coming year. The market has been relatively depressed, but there are signs of recovery. There is uncertainty about the speed of recovery of consumer expenditure, an uncertainty which is reinforced by the knowledge that consumers are currently holding relatively large liquid balances. Several forecasts have been made by the various forecasting agencies, but they tend to group around three tendencies, 4, 8 and 11 per cent growth over the current year's levels. The marketing manager calculates what each of these consumer expenditure growth rates will imply for his sales, given certain assumptions about market share, prices, and so on. He derives the optimum stock-building policy (taking into account stock holding costs etc.) for each of these growth rates (note that he could also choose to investigate intermediate policies which are not optimum for any one of the growth rates). These are expressed in terms of the level of stock at the beginning of the heavy buying season, because once the season starts, even the lowest rate of growth of consumer expenditure will not allow him to build stock during the season. He then calculates the profitability of each policy under different growth rates and arrives at the Figures in Table 3.2. From this table, a regret matrix (a table of the costs of incorrect decisions) can be constructed (the bracketed figures), showing the difference between the profit actually made for each combination of stock policy and growth rate and the profit that could have been made if the stock policy had been optimally adjusted to the growth rate. The regret minimiser will choose the medium stock policy, because this will always (under the assumptions made) put the firm within $50,000 of the highest profit that could have been made, if stock had been optimally adjusted. The regret minimiser does not want to pay too high a cost for making an incorrect decision. He prefers to hedge his bets.

TABLE 3.2   Profitability ($ thousand)

Stock-building policy	Consumer expenditure increase		
	4%	8%	11%
High	300(100)	400(50)	550(0)
Medium	350(50)	450(0)	500(50)
Low	400(0)	400(50)	400(150)

Regret minimising behaviour can lead to the pursuit of parallel strategies. Several strategies[6] are followed, each aimed at achieving the same end result. However, such a policy may come into conflict with a firm's profit aims because distributing research or marketing effort over different fields of activity may lead to higher expected profitability.

Company and management attitudes to risk and uncertainty The problem of the individual marketing manager is to make his decisions in a rational way, such that he can justify them to himself and to his company. In order to do this, he needs to analyse his own and his company's attitude to risk and uncertainty. There may well be divergence between the attitude implied by company aims and the attitude that is consistent with the manager's personal aims. For example, reinforcing chances of promotion may depend on the achievement of a major policy success, and this may lead to a manager opting for a policy which is riskier than is consistent with company aims because there is a chance that it will produce the major success he needs. It is therefore important for marketing management to work out the implications of their company's aims by evaluating risk and uncertainty in every policy area. This implies analysing the spill-over effects of marketing policy (e.g. on liquidity, production and, of course, corporate strategy) to see how marketing risk affects overall company risk. Sensitivity analysis should be used not only *within* marketing analysis, to show how marketing policy decisions are affected by different assumptions about demand, costs and other aspects of the business environment, but also to show how overall company performance is affected by success or failure in particular marketing policies. This applies particularly where key determinant variables in particular analyses cannot be forecast and no surrogates can be found. If possible, simulation techniques should be used to analyse the impact of marketing risk on company risk.

MULTI-STAGE DECISIONS

In Chapter 2 we used the notion of tree-like structure of decisions (p. 18). Each decision may lead to any of several outcomes, each of which requires that another decision be made. If we can assign probabilities and values to each of the outcomes, then starting at the branches which are farthest from the starting point, we can evaluate each branch and thence the whole 'tree'. We can evaluate a set of decisions using criteria other than expected value (for instance risk minimisation at certain stages). We can also simulate such sets of decisions by using the decision criteria as inputs and changing the information inputs accordingly. Even if such sophisticated analyses are rendered impossible by the lack of appropriate information, setting up the framework helps to clarify the structure of the problem.

DECISION ANALYSIS: CONCLUSIONS

In this chapter, we have considered some aspects of the logic of decision analysis. We have seen that there are certain problem areas that need to be taken into account, in particular the nature of the data, the fitting of the analysis to the targets of the firm, and dealing with risk and uncertainty. In the policy chapters of this book (Chapters 8 onwards), we consider the practical implications of some of these points. First, however, we consider information inputs into marketing decisions.

4 The Economy

If we define the marketing manager's job as that of structuring the relations between the firm and its customers, it is clear that in order to do the job successfully the manager needs to be well informed about the firm and its environment (buyers, distributors, competitors, resource usage inside the firm, etc.). Information about these areas needs to be obtained and interpreted without too much expenditure of time and resources. In Chapters 4–7, we separate those parts of economic analysis which may be of use to the marketing manager in extracting information from his environment and interpreting it.

Economic analysis tends to be based on information derived from observation of behaviour in the recent past. When we use such analyses for forecasting purposes, we face certain problems. First, we have to forecast the values of variables which we have established as being determinants of the variable in which we are interested. Second, we should have some indication that the relationship that existed in the past between the variables investigated is likely to continue in the period for which we are forecasting. The relationships we are interested in relate to human behaviour. Success in prediction depends on correct modelling of this behaviour and on being able to obtain the right information. In most cases, we are forced to compromise. The most important reason for compromising is that data may be either impossible or very expensive to obtain. Where this is so, we may use models which do not take into account all the variables which in principle affect the situation being modelled. Changes in excluded variables may take place which significantly alter behaviour patterns and therefore make a particular model (which seemed to account well for past behaviour) inappropriate. The stability of relationships established in this way therefore depends upon changes of this kind not occurring.

Successful marketing requires the analysis and use of many kinds of information, ranging from general information about the state of the world economy to specific information about the demand for a given brand and the costs of producing a given product. Economics can make two general kinds of contribution here: the producing of a model of determination of a variable and the quantifying of that model. The two are highly interdependent. Without familiarity with the subject matter, serious mistakes can be made in quantifying a particular model and in interpreting the results of the quantification.

In making a decision, a manager may start with a relatively limited information requirement. In deciding how to price a new product, analysis may start with the effect of the prices of competing products, how buyers have responded to them, what the effect of promotional expenditure has been, cost and capacity information and other items closely related to the product itself. However, the price that can be obtained depends partly on the general competitive situation in the industry, what is happening to overall demand for the product class, how this is affected by the overall economic situation, and so on. The marketing manager is unlikely to carry out his own analysis of all these factors (although certain firms do construct aggregate economic models for their own use). The more general the information, the more likely the manager is to rely upon published sources, consultants, etc. However, if marketing management can come to grips with the models on which they are dependent for information or analysis, they should be able to improve the efficiency and discrimination with which they use the models. For this reason, we start our discussion of methods of analysis at a relatively general level, turning to more specific topics in the following two chapters.

THE WORLD ECONOMY

The buoyancy of the world economy affects the buoyancy of many national economies and hence the demand for products within them. Many companies use information derived from analysis of the world economy as inputs into decisions on long-run market choice, on the source of raw materials and on location of sales and manufacturing facilities. For marketing purposes, the level of aggregate demand in the world economy is likely to interest only the very largest multinational companies. However, more specific aspects of the world economy are often taken directly into account in marketing decisions. Here we consider three examples: exchange rates, the terms of trade and trade blocs.

EXCHANGE RATES

Many firms, even if they are not directly involved in international trade and are located within relatively self-sufficient economies (such as the US), find their marketing analyses affected by exchange rate changes, especially when governments allow rates to change frequently. Markets where there is only a little import competition can quickly be turned into markets where imports take a large market share or where prices have to be adjusted downwards to counter the import threat, because of changes in exchange parities. Producers who export little may find major market opportunities opening up as a result of such changes. One problem marketing management faces in this respect is to decide whether parity movements are likely to continue in the same direction, justifying long-term policy changes, or whether they are transient and should be ridden out (e.g. by accepting lower profit margins or reaping higher ones without any change in marketing policy, apart from minor switching of output between markets). This problem is complicated in some countries by 'dirty' floating (intervention in foreign exchange markets, which are in principle free, in order to achieve short-term policy aims) or by the accumulation of substantial foreign exchange reserves, leading to speculation about changes in the form in which they are held and consequent moves in exchange rates irrespective of trade and investments flows and relative price and productivity movements.

The basic determinants of exchange rates include actual and expected flows of trade (goods and services) and investment, public and private transfers of other kinds, switches in currency holdings, relative price and productivity movements, and of course expectations concerning the determinants of such factors. Economies which are in substantial deficit on their trading account may have stable exchange rates because of balancing incoming investment flows or government intervention to maintain parities.[1] For a large part of the post-war period, the US ran a substantial surplus on trading account, balanced mainly by a substantial outflow of investment funds (which incidentally helped solve world liquidity problems for some time).

Let us consider an example of the kind of problem marketing management may face as a result of exchange rate changes and how economic analysis may help to sort out policy alternatives. Consider the position of a US manufacturer of advanced machine tools who exports a substantial proportion of his turnover to advanced industrial markets. In the late 1970s, the US dollar starts to depreciate fairly rapidly against major world currencies, while the West German mark (the domestic currency of some of his major competitors) appreciates to some extent against most currencies, including the US dollar. The marketing vice-president is considering the implications of these changes for his current and long-term marketing policies. He reasons in the following way.

There are three reasons for the depreciation of the US dollar. The first is that the role of the dollar as a reserve currency is being taken over, at least in part, by other currencies such as the German mark, the Swiss franc and the Japanese yen. As long as this continues, a fall in the dollar relative to these currencies is to be expected, because the process is a result of an increased willingness to hold these currencies and a reduced willingness to hold the dollar. Once the process is over, parities will reflect other trade, capital and price movements. However, the process brings about the need for readjustment in the respective economies. For example, the US will not be able to continue to supply the expanding demand for international liquidity by running a deficit on current or capital account. This will intensify the effects of the other two factors.

The second reason for the depreciation of the dollar is that inflation in the US is higher than in some key industrial nations. This leads to depreciation of a free-floating dollar because US goods and services become relatively expensive and get priced out of markets, leading to a fall in demand for the dollar, unless the exchange rate depreciates to counter this. The depreciation of the dollar caused by inflation does not affect all exporters equally. Rising input prices can be offset to some extent by increased factor productivity. The individual firm can 'beat' inflation if it manages to increase productivity fast enough. Those firms which can maintain the value of a dollar spent on their output will benefit in export markets by the depreciation of the dollar. Firms with average productivity growth rates will find themselves more or less in the same position, while firms with lower than average productivity growth rates will find selling more difficult. In other words, inflation and associated exchange rate changes may affect the efficiency with which the price-based mechanism for transferring output between more and less efficient firms works. In the absence of inflation, downward price inflexibility may hamper this mechanism.

The marketing vice-president might reason that if productivity growth in his firm is relatively slow, then the long-run prospects for his firm in export markets are weak, and further depreciation of the dollar will not solve the problem. If total industry productivity is growing slowly, then losing markets despite depreciation of the dollar may be the beginning of a long process of attrition which results in the death of an industry in one country and its transfer to another.

The second cause of the depreciation of the dollar is the substantial rise in the value of US imports following the large increases in oil prices that took place in the 1970s. Apart from having an inflationary impact and affecting the structure of energy industries and energy-related or dependent industries, it also affects the balance between domestic and foreign production and consumption. Unless the tendency to consume oil is reduced, then some major switches in the pattern of activity will have to take place in the economy to pay for the oil. These switches will be encouraged by the depreciation of the dollar. Import substitution and export industries will benefit from the depreciation of the dollar which will take place until the economy has adjusted to the higher oil price.

In considering the effect of the parity changes on his main competitors, the marketing vice-president may reason in the following way. The relatively low rate of inflation in West Germany increases the value of the mark in terms of other currencies. The success of German export industries, which continued during the period of appreciation of the mark (suggesting that previous success was not due to earlier under-valuation of the mark), produced substantial export surpluses, encouraging the rise of the mark. This impairs the competitiveness of parts of the German machine tool industry, but in certain product areas they have established such a strong reputation for quality and reliability that price differentials have had no impact. However, in more price-sensitive markets, there will be increased opportunities for the US firm. Market segmentation analysis will have to be used to isolate appropriate markets.

The conclusion of this analysis may be that there is a major market opportunity opening up in markets which are currently major buyers of West German machinery. This opportunity may persist for several years as US consumers are showing some reluctance to change their consumption habits (implying a continuation of the import surplus problem). The burden of the adjustment is therefore likely to fall on the export industries. The mark is likely to continue to appreciate because of the slow rate of reduction of the German import surplus, and although rapid productivity advances on the part of the German engineering industry will help to keep prices down,[2] this will not be enough to stop their relative prices rising.

TERMS OF TRADE

The terms of trade are defined as the relation between a country's export prices and import prices. The importance of the terms of trade, for which there are various other measures,[3] is that they indicate a country's purchasing power in international markets (together with the total amount of exports). The purchasing capacity of customer countries depends partly upon the amount they export, the amount of purchasing power that is transferred to them and the prices they can get for their exports.

Terms of trade depend upon a variety of factors. If monetary factors can be assumed to have no real influence except through any transfer of purchasing power (that is to say, excluding any effect caused by inflation and the exchange rate being out of line), then the main determinants of the terms of trade are production and supply conditions (in particular the consequences for unit costs of expansion or contraction of the output of traded goods and the relative importance of the countries concerned as suppliers of particular traded goods), demand conditions (in particular the relative importance of countries as customers) and various factors which affect demand and supply (for example, natural factors such as climate and resource bases, technology, etc.

There are certain points in the analysis of terms of trade which have particular relevance for marketing analysis. An example of this is the hypothesis of the secular deterioration of the terms of trade of developing countries. If this were true,[4] it would imply that the economic growth of developing countries would not lead to a proportionate expansion of their import markets. In general, strategic marketing analysis should take into account expected movements in the terms of trade.

TRADE BLOCS AND COMMON MARKETS

If a preferential trading area (in which members reduce barriers to imports from other members) is set up, markets within the area may change in size and nature. The effects may range from changes in production and consumption patterns to changes in payments balances and the rate of economic growth. Production may be shifted from lower cost sources outside the area to higher cost sources within the area. This can reduce real income levels and the size of markets (except for producers of such products located within the area), unless it facilitates the employment of resources which were previously unemployed. Production may also be shifted from high cost sources within the area to lower cost sources within the same area. This will increase income and market size (except for the high cost producers). These shifts and the associated consumption shifts will have terms of trade and balance of payments effects. These 'static' effects may be accompanied by 'dynamic' effects of increased competition – stimulating efficiency and increasing income – and increased exploitation of economies of scale, although there is some argument on this question.[5] In firms which are involved in any way in markets where trade blocs are being created, it is important to take all the above factors into account in formulating long-term marketing policy.

DEVELOPMENT AND GROWTH OF NATIONAL MARKETS

For short and long-term marketing planning, it is important to analyse the likely development of economies in which the firm is involved. There are two basic (interrelated) ways of analysing national economies. *Macroeconomic* analysis deals with aggregate demand and supply in the economy and the way in which they interact, taking into account the impact of economic relations with other countries. Using assumptions concerning the behaviour of key economic groups, quantified macroeconomic analysis can produce forecasts of the level of activity in the economy and in its component parts for the short to medium term (say up to five years). Another way of looking at economies is to consider changes in their structure. The more structural perspective of *development economics* is important for marketing analysis of economies which are undergoing rapid structural change; relationships which standard macroeconomic analysis reveal as being roughly constant in developed economies may change substantially enough in developing economies to affect the level of activity of the economy as a whole and the size of particular markets within it.

MACROECONOMIC ANALYSIS

Macroeconomic analysis as standardly carried out[6] is a highly sophisticated analysis of demand and supply at the aggregate, national level. Demand is broken down into its various components (including public and private consumption, capital formation and export demand). The determinants of each component are then analysed. Supply of goods and services is equal to the output of all domestic industries plus import supply. Since production of this output creates income and since several of the demand components are heavily dependent on income (in particular, private consumption), national income is taken to be the prime equilibrating variable in the system (although monetary variables may have a considerable equilibrating effect under certain conditions).

In this system, the immediate focus of interest for marketers is the flow of demand which relates to their own markets. For manufacturers of consumer goods or of inputs into their production, consumer demand is the main item of interest. For capital equipment manufacturers, public and private (non-household) capital formation are the most important items. Construction industries may be more interested in household capital formation (mostly demand for new houses) and public capital formation (which contains a major element of public construction projects). Because forecasts of these components of demand are often the basic input into marketing planning information systems, it is important to understand the analysis that lies behind the forecasts.

CONSUMPTION DEMAND

For medium to long-term marketing purposes, consumption demand can be regarded as dependent principally on personal disposable income, defined as personal income (wages, salaries, dividends and rents) less government levies on it (income tax, social security contributions, etc.). Although from year to year there may be variations in the consumption ratio (the ratio of consumption expenditure to personal disposable income), time-series studies over long periods indicate a high constancy of the consumption ratio,[7] at least in developed nations. Over shorter periods, especially within business cycles, the consumption ratio tends to fluctuate, rising as income falls and falling as income rises. Cross-sectional evidence also shows that individuals save a higher proportion of their disposable income as that income increases. This raises questions about the capacity of consumers to find ways of spending their money as they become better off.

Various attempts have been made to explain the apparent discrepancy between time-series and cross-sectional findings of studies on the consumption ratio. Duesenberry's relative income hypothesis[8] suggests that individuals' consumption depends not on their absolute income but on their income relative to that of others. The higher an individual's income relative to others, the smaller the proportion of it he will spend on consumption compared with others. As long as he remains in the same relative income position, he will continue to spend the same proportion of his income on consumption, no matter how much the overall level of income rises in the economy. If individuals with rising relative incomes are offset by individuals with falling relative incomes, the aggregate consumption ratio will stay the same. If this is a correct representation of the situation, it suggests that although the relatively well-off may save a higher proportion of their income, they will go on increasing their consumption expenditure at the same rate as their income increases, implying that their wants do not become saturated. The behavioural basis of the hypothesis should be the individual's *perception* of his relative position, rather than his actual relative position. This might account for the cyclical behaviour of the consumption ratio. In an upswing, more consumers consider themselves relatively better off and thus spend a lower proportion of their increased income. This hypothesis is worth bearing in mind for marketing analysis in periods when substantial groups of consumers change their relative income position.[9]

Another view of the relationship between consumption demand and income is that consumption adjusts slowly and continuously to changes in income. This idea was first investigated in detail by Brown,[10] although Friedman's work on it is the best known.[11] Just as consumers may show inertia in brand choice, so they may show inertia in their expenditure pattern when conditions change. Friedman employed the notions of *transitory* and *permanent* income. Measured income can be considered to be made up of a permanent component (which the consumer considers to be his normally available income) and a transitory component (the rest of his measured income). If measured income is less than permanent income, the transitory component will be negative. Friedman hypothesises that consumers react differently to changes in permanent income and changes in transitory income, the proportion of transitory income saved being higher than that of permanent income. This means that a consumer whose income is above his permanent income will have a lower than usual consumption ratio, while if his income is below his permanent income, he will have a higher than usual consumption ratio. Finally, transitory income is slowly converted into permanent income, implying that an addition to income will first have a relatively high savings component, but if the addition persists it will be counted entirely as permanent income and be spent in the same proportion as the original permanent income.

This theory is partially supported by cross-sectional and time-series evidence.[12] Its significance for marketing management lies in its interpretation of the effects of major changes in national income, which we would not expect to be translated into the same proportionate change in consumption immediately. This inertia may be more noticeable with some products than with others. Items of consumer expenditure which require major outlays over a period (because they are financed over a period or because they entail maintenance, annual taxes, etc.) may be the last to respond to income increases.

Other major determinants of consumption demand include financial conditions, liquid assets and wealth. The availability and terms of consumer finance is regulated by the authorities in many countries. Sudden relaxation of credit restrictions can lead to a substantial bringing forward of expenditure, not just in the industries producing goods bought on credit but also (through the multiplier effect) in other industries. Consumer durables are especially sensitive to finance conditions because they often represent an outlay which consumers cannot finance out of current income. Empirically, consumers seem to be divisible into credit users and non-credit users,[13] a point which marketing analysis should take into account through appropriate segmentation.

Liquid assets are an important subdivision of wealth. They can be unloaded suddenly, producing a rise in consumer expenditure which is unrelated to income levels. Although most studies of the effect of liquid assets on consumption using annual data show that the effect is insignificant, this is probably accounted for by the deficiencies of using annual data (years of unloading of assets of goods show low liquidity and high consumption).[14] Rather than considering the effect to be on aggregate consumption, it is probably better to picture the consumer as switching between various forms of asset as financial conditions change. High liquid assets are important in marketing analysis because they are an indication of capacity to 'unload' expenditure. Whether reasons for unloading are financial (for example reduction in yields on liquid assets, relaxation of consumer finance, etc.) or related to expectations about the state of the economy is a matter for further analysis.

Wealth is used to smooth out fluctuations in income, whether short-term (for example as a result of the business cycle) or long-term (for example over the course of an individual's lifetime). The notion of the consumer as a rational allocator of expenditure and saving between periods which may span as long an interval as a lifetime was analysed by Modigliani.[15] Wealth accumulation is seen as the result of a series of decisions about how to allocate resources among periods. The marketing implication of this view is that the effect of wealth on expenditure depends on a consumer's life-cycle position, apart from any natural sequence of consumer durable acquisition (which will be reflected in wealth figures). Moreover expectations about the future will affect the consumer's desire to increase or run-down his wealth (to save more or less, in other words).

As well as affecting wealth accumulation decisions, expectations may affect consumption more directly. Studies carried out by Katona and others have shown exceptional variables (such as expectations about the overall level of economic activity, price rises, and unemployment) to be of some importance in explaining expenditure, particularly on consumer durables.[16] Expectational variables are more important in explaining short-run fluctuations in expenditure than long-run variations. They also may be difficult to predict (and therefore of limited usefulness in forecasting) or dependent on other, more forecastable variables (which can be used themselves).[17]

INVESTMENT DEMAND

Capital equipment is not demanded for its own sake but as an input into a production process. The decision to buy extra capital equipment depends on the demand for the output which can be produced with it and whether capacity exists to supply it, as well as on the cost of buying and financing the equipment, the rate of depreciation of existing equipment and the amount of equipment there is to depreciate. Demand for investment goods is an important factor not just for manufacturers of capital equipment. As a major, relatively fluctuating variable which is partly independent of the level of current economic activity, investment demand exerts a strong influence on the overall level of economic activity.

In analysing the demand for capital equipment, the capital–output ratio of the economy is often assumed to be fixed.[18] This implies that a given proportional expansion in the output of the economy will always require the same proportional increase in capital stock (assuming existing stock to be fully employed). Although some constancy has been found in average capital–output ratios in various economies, this should not be relied upon for analysis of marginal changes in output. Capital is only one of the inputs into the production process. As the relative prices of inputs change, so the proportions in which they are combined may change. Although at the aggregate level change is likely to be slow, when expansion or contraction of output does take place we should expect any change in relative prices of inputs to affect the ratios in which inputs are used and this will affect the market for capital goods.

Changes in technology also affect the capital–output ratio. Technological advance may involve completely new production processes, reducing or increasing capital–output ratios. Changes may also occur in the productivity of capital goods industries, such that existing kinds of production equipment can be produced more cheaply. Whether this leads to more capital being substituted for labour depends upon relative prices of capital and labour and on technical substitutability.

Even if the capital–output ratio could reasonably be assumed to be fixed, because investment plans are dependent on past and expected future levels of economic activity, the relationship between investment demand and aggregate output is a complex one.[19] Because expectations are often extrapolated from past trends, a lagged relationship is implied.[20] Because investment is partially dependent on past economic activity and itself is a major determinant of the aggregate level of activity, once an increase in that level begins, it may be accelerated by the investment process.[21] Once investment expenditure starts to rise (either because of an accumulation of depreciation which can no longer be deferred or because it has been encouraged by an increase in aggregate demand which took place for some other reason), income is created in the investment goods industries. This is spent partly on consumer goods, creating more demand for the output of the firms which buy investment goods. In turn firms in the investment goods industries will buy more equipment, and the process accelerates (for an increase in output will normally require more than an equivalent increase in output in the capital goods industries and leakages from the circular flow of income are unlikely to depress the process enough) until firms begin to reach full capacity production. At this stage, order backlogs start to build up and demand may be channelled into imports or create inflation. The reverse process can also occur.

The nature of the above relationship is affected by the existence of spare capacity in both final goods and investment goods industries. Spare capacity may result from a straightforward overall shortage of equipment or from the fact that available equipment is of the wrong technical kind (for example outdated and expensive to operate), in the wrong physical location, in the wrong firm (for example in a firm which is losing market share) and so on. The existence of substantial aggregate excess capacity does not prevent considerable non-depreciation investment taking place. However, successful marketing of investment goods in times of aggregate excess capacity may require careful market segmentation and a more competitive marketing policy.

If we assume that investment decisions are based on an assessment of the profits to be made by investing, then the yield of the investment and the cost of making it should determine whether it will be undertaken.[22]

The yield depends upon the increase in the value of output (or in cost saving) that the investment makes possible, together with the increase in costs of associated inputs. The cost of acquiring the equipment itself can be separated into the actual purchase price and the cost of financing the purchase. Purchase price changes depend mainly on productivity, factor costs and competition in the capital goods industries. As we have noted, their effect is likely to be stronger in periods of overall changes in activity levels.

As far as the cost of finance is concerned, we should expect firms to have a portfolio of projects under consideration at any one time, and their choice of projects to be affected by the cost of borrowing to finance equipment to be used in particular projects (or by the opportunity cost of retained profits used for this purpose). A fall in the cost of capital would make a larger number of projects viable, in particular those with yields distributed more strongly in the medium to long-term range. In practice, although a lower cost of capital does produce some increase in investment demand, there is also evidence (in particular from business attitude surveys) of some insensitivity to changes in the cost of finance.[23] This implies that cheaper finance cannot always be relied upon to increase investment demand. Responses differ from firm to firm, depending on the source of capital, the size of the firm, the nature of its business and the style of management. Also, we should expect the relationship between investment demand and the cost of capital to be less direct because of planning and implementation lags. The delay may be longer than that typical between demand and investment changes, where the delay is subject to reduction because of anticipation of demand increases. Changes in the cost of capital are more difficult to foresee.

The size of capital stock is an important determinant of investment demand. It has a twofold effect. The first effect is through the relationship between demand for final output and capital stock (the capital–output ratio). If the capital stock is insufficient to meet existing or anticipated demand for final output, then investment is likely to rise. The second part of the effect is through the age distribution of capital stock. Capital stock depreciates over time, and as long as demand for final output is maintained, a substantial proportion of the demand for capital equipment will normally be a demand for the renewal of equipment. The size of this demand depends on the size of capital stock and its age distribution. Replacement is deferrable, so anticipation of a depression will cause it to be deferred, while anticipation of an upswing will cause it to be brought forward. The age distribution of capital stock may be uneven as a result of past bunching of investment. Depending on the average life of equipment, replacement cycles may be strong enough to pull industries and economies out of a depression.

Because investment and capital stock tends to be concentrated in fewer firms than output in general, demand forecasting in investment goods markets may be able to rely on study of the behaviour of a few firms, their reactions to interest rate changes, to changes in profitability and their expectations concerning the future behaviour of the economy. The behaviour of relatively few large firms may determine the output of substantial parts of the investment goods industries and hence the level of output of the economy as a whole. The confidence of such firms in the future performance of the economy can therefore exert a major influence on economic trends.

Various indices of business confidence (from those based on specially designed questionnaires to ones based on stock market indices) have been analysed to look for effects on investment demand. There is some evidence that expectations about future demand levels tend to be based on rather unsophisticated extrapolations of the past.[24] When a firm's actual investment expenditure differs significantly from its expressed intentions, it tends to be because of changes in sales and earnings and because of incorrect or incomplete anticipations (with delays in construction and deliveries exerting some influence).[25] This suggests that although expectations may be important in fixing investment plans, the plans themselves may be altered in the light of current changes in the economic environment of the firm. It is interesting to note that although stock prices do not influence investment in any straightforward way, there is some indication that they act as a proxy for expected output.[26] Stock price changes may therefore be a useful indicator of customer prospects.

Inventory investment is an important element of a firm's total investment. Suppliers of raw materials and of semi-finished goods often face severe problems in the periods of rapid stock-building which occur in anticipation of a boom or in the periods of cut-backs on stocks which occur in anticipation of a depression. Empirical evidence suggests that if 75 per cent of the fluctuations in inventory investment could have been controlled, the US would not have had *any* post-war business recessions![27] Use of aggregate inventory statistics should therefore help to improve marketing planning significantly. Timing of the introduction of new products, new developments in distribution, and so on, should be adjusted in the light of what is happening to aggregate inventories. However, inventory behaviour needs to be interpreted with care.

Inventories are held and acquired for several reasons.[28] The accumulation of inventories may not be a sign of increased *demand* for inventories but rather the result of an involuntary accumulation of stocks because of an unexpected fall in the demand for final output. Inventory statistics should therefore be analysed in conjunction with final demand information. However, manufacturers may increase their inventories deliberately despite a fall in demand for final output if final demand is expected to pick up again; in this case the inventories are being used as a buffer stock. This kind of behaviour is particularly common in industries where there are marked cycles in demand (for instance seasonal industries). Correspondingly, a fall in inventories when final demand increases may just represent the use of inventories as a buffer stock.

Inventories are held principally for transactions purposes. Inventories of a firm's own input requirements are held to reduce the need for too frequent transactions with suppliers, to reduce the risk of being out of stock of particular materials because of delays in supply, to ease quality control procedures, and so on. Inventories of finished output are held to reduce problems of trying to synchronise problems with demand, to take advantage of economies of scale, and so on. The ratio between the transactions demand for inventories and the level of output normally remains fairly constant, being relatively unaffected by factors such as interest rates and company liquidity, at least at the aggregate level. From the marketing point of view, the important source of changes here is through expectations about the level of final demand. Increased optimism may produce a sudden rise in the demand for stocks.

The speculative motive for holding stocks is that which is determined by factors such as expectations about changes in the level of prices or in the availability of produce. This kind of speculation is likely to be significant at the national level when major destabilising factors (war, signs of major change in government policy on taxes or trade, rapid inflation when no other assets are available to firms as ways of holding liquidity) are present. When aggregate speculation does occur, it can destroy the best laid marketing plans and its possibility should therefore be taken into account.

EXPORT AND IMPORT DEMAND

From the point of view of the national economy, import demand represents a leakage of expenditure from the domestic market, while export demand represents an injection of expenditure. Export and import demand have consumption, investment and government expenditure elements which are determined by the factors described above. Additional determinants include differences between countries in prices (affected by movements in productivity, inflation and exchange rates, as well as tariffs and subsidies), natural influences (distance, taste differences and so on) and government regulations (health and safety, for example). The basic method of foreign trade analysis differs from that for one country only in its multi-country nature and by the increased significance of relative prices. We consider some special factors in Chapter 9.

PUBLIC OR GOVERNMENT DEMAND

Public authorities vary in their importance from economy to economy. They are important for marketing analysis because they both absorb and transfer resources. Both of these actions can affect the aggregate level of demand. For example, transferring spending power from the high income groups (high savers) to low income groups (low savers) will normally increase consumer demand. Absorbing more resources through, say, increased public investment will increase demand for investment goods. The government may prevent absorption of resources by individuals (and therefore reduce demand) by increasing taxation and neither transferring nor spending the proceeds.

The government usually assumes the role of regulator of the macroeconomic system. If the way the economy is going is likely to produce unacceptable levels of unemployment, inflation, trade deficit or investment outflow, then the government may use its policy instruments (for example taxation, public expenditure, interest rates, monetary controls, trade controls) to alter the course of the economy. The marketer's problem is not only that of understanding the effect of government policies on the economy, nor that of comprehending the semi-political arguments for intervention. It is that of trying to forecast which way the system is likely to move under current policies and what the government is likely to do to change the course of the system. It cannot be assumed that the authorities will follow some optimal policy, given their aims, because they too have severe information problems. They may act too early or too late, and do too much or too little, to achieve their aims. Much of the post-war experience of the UK is that of governments persistently doing too much too late to cure depressions or overheating and then having to act again to cure the ills that the overstimulation or excessive braking caused.[29] In other words, turning points in aggregate activity were consistently misjudged. However, in the 1960s and 1970s governments have become more moderate in the use of brake and accelerator, and forecasting procedures and judgements have become considerably more open. Marketers would benefit from paying some attention to the debate about forecasting procedures and to comparisons of the results of different forecasting institutions.

Monetary aspects The impact of money and credit on the 'real' economy (the output of and demand for the volume of goods and services) is rather complex. Monetary conditions (the supply of money and credit, the rate of inflation, etc.) affect the level of aggregate demand in several ways. Whether this be through interaction among the rate of interest, investment demand and income levels in investment goods industries and national income, or through interaction among inflation, business uncertainty, investment and national income, or a more straightforward money supply–aggregate demand linkage, it is worth the marketer's while to keep informed on monetary developments.

THE ANALYSIS OF ECONOMIC DEVELOPMENT

The evolution of the size and nature of purchasing power depends on how an economy develops. Purchasing power produces markets, and the basic criterion of purchasing power is income per head. The long-run determinants of income per head include:

1. population (dependent on birth, mortality, immigration and emigration rates);
2. hours worked (dependent on labour force participation rates, length of working week, number of holidays, amount of overtime worked, time lost through industrial stoppages, etc.);
3. productivity of labour (dependent on skill and education level of workforce, amount of other inputs available per worker, technologies used, work habits, etc.);
4. amount of capital used (determined by past levels of investment, rates of depreciation, appropriateness of past investments, etc.);
5. productivity of capital (determined by technology embodied in equipment, amount of other inputs used with capital, intensity of use of equipment, etc.);
6. amount of land available for productive use (determined by geo-

graphical area, natural features, amount of reclamation undertaken, etc.);

7. productivity of land (determined by natural characteristics, past investments in improving productivity, climatic conditions, amount of other factors combined with land, etc.);
8. foreign transfers of resources (e.g. foreign aid, investment);
9. world prices of inputs into and outputs of the economy (terms of trade).

Instead of considering each of these factors in detail, we shall try to show by example how analysis of growth and development can provide information for marketing planning.

Consider the position of a manufacturer of nitrates and phosphates of various kinds. His products have a wide range of uses, from fertilisers, animal feed additives and human food preservatives to metal treatment compounds. His agricultural products are more suited to intensive modes of farming, his human food preservatives are suited to pre-packed products and his metal treatment products to pre-treatment of surfaces to be given a high quality paint finish. In general, his products are suited to countries in the more advanced stages of economic development without large areas of high quality land.

In approaching his marketing analysis, the marketing manager of the company assumes that he cannot afford to analyse only those economies which have already reached the more advanced stages of economic development, because in these countries, competition to supply his type of products is intense. He therefore wants to identify those countries which are likely to exhibit faster rates of economic growth starting from situations of relative underdevelopment. To economise on research effort, he selects for analysis those countries which have exhibited rapid rates of growth over the last few years in the agricultural, packaged food and engineering sectors. He then considers how these economies are likely to evolve over the next ten years and how this is likely to affect the markets in which he is interested.

He starts with the agricultural sector in each economy, examines the trend in world demand and supply and world prices for the principal commodities produced by the economy. Long-run decline in the sales or price of a major commodity coupled with an absence of flexibility in changing the commodity base is a bad sign, because it may indicate an impoverishment of agriculture rather than progress and hence lack of market for advanced agricultural inputs. Consolidation of holdings together with indications that farmers are willing and able to switch crops is interpreted as a good sign. He also takes into account the extent to which industrialisation is drawing people off the land, setting higher objectives for income and wealth for the population, allowing more consolidation of holdings to take place and producing a greater demand for convenience foods. Another factor which he takes into account is the level of education amongst agricultural entrepreneurs. The higher the level, the more they are able to understand the advantages of using more advanced fertilisers and feed additives. He also takes into account the rate of development of the agricultural infrastructure, for this determines the ability of agriculture to handle the production and distribution of higher value crops and the ease of distribution of fertilisers and feed additives. The rate of investment in agriculture is also analysed, in particular whether profits (if any) are being invested in land improvement, building up herds, etc., whether credit facilities are available and accessible, and so forth. If large families are dependent on the yields of small areas for their livelihood, this is likely to absorb profits and reduce investment. In general, he tries to establish whether there is a tendency towards more efficient, more intensive exploitation of land and whether such a tendency is likely to continue.

In his analysis of the prospects for the engineering industry, the marketing manager first considers the general progress of the manufacturing sector and then its influence on the engineering industries through capital investment, labour market, infrastructure development and so on. The engineering industries' product lines and production trends are examined, with particular emphasis on adaptability to changes in the type of product demanded, rates of investment, profitability and dependence on government aid. The skill and education levels of the population are assessed in order to establish the extent to which industries are able to absorb new kinds of equipment and technologies. The infrastructure (transport, sources of investment, etc.) is also taken into account. In general, the marketing manager is trying to assess the buoyancy of the engineering industries in conditions of changing demand and technology.

The evolution of the pre-packed foods sector is analysed in terms of the growth in per capita income. Demographic factors (such as urbanisation) and social factors (which determine degree of acceptability of pre-packed foods) are also taken into account. The distribution industry plays an important role because it both promotes and is dependent on the supply of pre-packed foods. The development of an appropriate distribution network in turn depends on degree of urbanisation, which determines the degree of concentration of buying power and hence the viability of more advanced modes of distribution. Countries which show high rates of advance of urbanisation together with high income growth are particularly good prospects.

ASSESSING THE IMPORTANCE OF DEVELOPMENT TRENDS

In short-run macroeconomic analysis, established techniques are available for estimating the importance of particular variables in determining the level of aggregate demand. As far as trends in economic development are concerned, although we may have no difficulty in picking out the variables which are likely to be important for particular marketing analyses, we do not usually have a ready-made framework for analysis. We are obliged to use a mixture of techniques: extensions of the standard macroeconomic analysis into the medium term, growth models which concentrate on the role of accumulation of capital (singling out investment and savings behaviour as key variables), input–output analysis with coefficients adjusted to allow for technical and structural change and econometric analyses aimed at establishing the importance of particular variables (e.g. education) on productivity and income. Comprehensive analysis of development entails using all these approaches, taking into account regional as well as national aspects. Such analyses are generally available in published form from the various international agencies (UN, OECD, etc.) and should provide the basic data input into market choice analysis.

ANALYSING THE ECONOMY: CONCLUSIONS

In this chapter, we have looked at some of the ways in which the working of the economy affects marketing planning and have suggested how information about the economy might be used. In practice, many firms use forecasts based on models which the user of the information does not understand as the basic inputs into their marketing decisions. As the providers of the models are not omniscient and not always the first to recognise their errors, it is important for marketing management to be able to assess models independently. This chapter has hopefully given an indication of where marketing can use understanding of the macro-economy.

5 Product Demand

There are two basic approaches to the analysis of demand. The first discusses the links between the quantity of a product demanded and variables such as price, income of buyer, advertising expenditure, and so on. The second approach, which is highly developed in the market research literature, analyses buyers' demand for product characteristics and how this demand is translated into demand for particular products (e.g. how demand for comfort, speed, acceleration capacity, etc. arises and is translated into demand for particular kinds of transport).

Fundamental to the first kind of approach is the notion of a demand function. A demand function states how the quantity of a product demanded is related to the variables which affect demand for it. The nature of the demand function depends upon which variables are included in the analysis, which in turn depends upon the nature of the product (including the breadth of its definition), the nature of its buyers and the nature of the marketing process for the product (including the competitive structure of the markets in which it is sold).

PRODUCT CHARACTERISTICS

The nature of demand analysis for a general product class (e.g. food) differs from that for a particular brand, because demand for the group, taken as a whole, is unlikely to be affected by competitive factors. For the analysis of demand for a general product class, it may be feasible to use input–output analysis. The basic rationale for input–output analysis is that demand for product classes (usually defined as the output of a complete industry) can be forecast by resolving it into final demand and intermediate demand, which is the demand by industry for the outputs of its own and other industries. Assuming that the composition of final demand (demand by consumers, by industry for investment goods and by public authorities for investment goods and for goods and services supplied for final use but not already included in the above categories) can be forecast by other techniques, then the demand for intermediate goods can be forecast if we know the relation between each industry's output and its demand for inputs from other industries. The coefficients that relate an industry's demand for the output of another industry to its own output are determined by technology employed, relative prices and a range of other variables. If we assume that the coefficients are fixed, then we can predict intermediate demand from final demand. It may be possible to include investment goods demand as intermediate demand rather than treating it as an exogenous variable, but the deferrability of investment between time periods suggests that its coefficients will not be stable enough for this. From the final demand for cars, we can predict the demand for steel by the motor industry itself, the demand for steel by industries supplying to the motor industry that arises from particular levels of production in the motor industry, and so on. The assumption of fixed coefficients limits the method to short-run forecasting use, and the breadth of definition of products limits the method to supplying industry forecasts. The method is most useful for providing basic input into industrial product demand forecasts.[1]

If the product in question is produced by a particular manufacturer and its sales can be influenced by marketing policy, then the kind of variables used in the analysis will include promotional expenditure by the firm and its competitors, relative prices, product quality and distributional strength. In the intermediate case of within-industry general product classes, where industry statistics may not permit the use of input–output analysis or where the product is a final product, the standard economic variables mentioned at the beginning of the chapter (price, income etc.) will be employed, together with product-specific variables. These include whether the good is a consumer or an industrial product, whether it is a service or a physical good, whether it is used only in special circumstances or only with certain other products, whether it is used as a substitute for other products, whether the product is new, and so forth.

BUYER CHARACTERISTICS

The standard economic picture of the buyer is that of a seeker of satisfaction (in the case of the individual consumer) or profitability (in the case of the industrial buyer). Given the circumstances in which most products are used, additional units of a product bought within a given time period yield less satisfaction or profitability, other things being equal, than the first units bought. This, together with the fact that most buyers operate under a purchasing budget constraint, implies that factors such as the relative price of the product, the purchasing budget of the buyer and the amount of the good already bought and stock held should be included in the analysis. In addition to these variables, there will be a range of buyer-specific variables that need to be included in the analysis: for example, location of buyer, social class, age possession of items used in conjunction with the product, management style (degree of delegation of purchasing decisions) and level of technical knowledge.

TIME

The variables included in a demand function depend upon the span of time over which we are trying to explain or predict demand. If we are trying to forecast demand for new cars over the coming month, then we do not include factors that are unlikely to change within a month or factors which, even if they do change, are unlikely to have any impact within a month. On the other hand, lagged values of such variables might be included because their effect is likely to be felt in the coming month. For such a short-term forecast, the main variables would probably be prices and consumer credit conditions (for private purchasers) and tax deduction or depreciation regulation changes (for company purchases). These variables can be changed significantly within a short period by administrative action; this can result in the bringing forward or deferring of purchases.

The time dimension is also important for new products, and in general for products where there is a secular growth or decline in demand. Unless the explanation for a secular demand trend can be found (for example income growth, time-dependent information diffusion process), then time may have to be included as an explicit but theoretically unconfirmed variable in the analysis.

Instead of relying on economic analysis to provide us with the appropriate list of variables, we could use the market research approach of trying to find out from buyers what kind of variables are likely to be important determinants of demand. This applies especially to product-specific and customer-specific variables. Because buying decisions depend upon buyers' perceptions of their own situations and of the characteristics of the range of products on offer, it may be worthwhile to carry out research on these points, especially if the product or market is one which is new to the buyer or to the firm (in which case, it may be risky to trust *a priori* reasoning as to which variables are likely to be important). Questionnaire results, appropriately analysed, should provide the data necessary for finding significantly different clusters of buyer characteristics. This aids the process of market segmentation. Market segments may be clearly enough defined and different enough in behaviour for demand analysis to be carried out separately for each segment. Questionnaire research should also help to isolate clusters of product characteristics which are considered important by buyers. This may help in determining quality variables for inclusion in the demand function.

MODELLING DEMAND

There are no general rules for modelling demand. The main tasks in modelling are defining the problem, identifying variables and representing them in a form that can be handled quantitatively. Here, we consider two examples of demand modelling, taking each with different breadths of product definition and over different time periods, from the standpoint of particular firms with specific marketing problems.

EXAMPLE 1: ACP, INC.

ACP is a US manufacturer of air-conditioning equipment. Its management is currently considering the firm's sales performance in the Australian market for split air-conditioning units. These have the advantage over standard wall-mounted units that the cooling unit can be mounted separately from the rest, reducing noise levels and allowing greater flexibility of location. ACP management wants to evaluate the short-term market, taking into account the growing success of Japanese competition, and also to establish the long-term prospects for the market.

The long run Air-conditioning units (like many consumer durables) have an income elasticity of demand in most markets which is greater than unity, so growth in per capita income will indicate good long-term prospects. This will be reinforced by buyers tending to switch away from the noisier and simpler wall units to split units as income rises (illustrating the tendency for income elasticities of demand to take more extreme values the closer the substitutes that are available). Some of the market for such units depends upon the construction of new housing and small institutional building (large institutions tending to go for central air conditioning). This market also grows with income, but fluctuates with construction cycles. The nature of the relation between per capita income and the demand for split units will change over time, as more smaller institutions may choose a central arrangement (as may larger private houses). Although there is likely to be a drawn-out process of diffusion of split units to lower income households, this effect may be neutralised by saturation appearing at higher income levels. Climatic factors produce inter-country differences in demand, as long as there is no change in the general climate in the country, this factor can be safely ignored. Vacation and business travel patterns may exercise an influence (through construction) on the demand for air-conditioning products in general, although hotel construction will mainly increase demand for central units. Another factor that may be of importance in the long term is the fall in the real price of split units (and of air-conditioning products in general) that is expected to take place as a result of product and production process improvements. This will lead to some broadening of the market. Factors that could militate against the development of the market include higher purchase tax rates, increased import duties, restrictions on consumer credit and other means of finance and higher real electricity prices.

From the above, we may derive that the following variables should be included in the long-run demand function for split units:

Disposable income
Distribution of income (for threshold and saturation analysis)
Building starts
Ownership of wall units
Ownership of split units
Relative prices of wall, split and central units
Purchase taxes and import duties
Consumer and commercial finance conditions
Electricity prices (relative to other energy prices)

Some of these variables may have to be excluded from long-term forecasts, however important anlysis of past data shows them to be, because of the impossibility of forecasting them. Income and its distribution can be forecast with as much certainty as most economic variables, although distribution may be sensitive to changes in personal tax rates and changes in relativities in times of inflation. Housing and other construction tends to be cyclical and dependent (with a lag) on finance and income. Ownership patterns can be forecast by rolling the demand forecast for this and other kinds of air conditioning one year forward at a time (although this requires separate modelling for other kinds of air conditioning). Price changes are difficult to forecast, since they are dependent on technological change and on the passing on of cost reductions to the buyer (dependent on competitive conditions). This applies both to the prices of air conditioning products and to electricity prices (the latter also depending on fuel prices and on government policies). Import duties, purchase taxation, finance rates and other government policy variables may be considered unforecastable for the purposes of this model. Variables which are considered unforecastable should not be ignored in initial quantitative analysis, for it is important to establish the sensitivity of the forecast to changes in unforecastable variables of the size that is likely to occur.

Once the variables for inclusion in the long-run model have been selected, the analysis needs to be quantified. Assuming that information on each variable is available, the remaining problems are those associated with the form of the function and the estimating procedure (see Chapter 7).

The short run In the short run, ACP is more concerned about the extent to which it can hold its own against Japanese competition. This means first establishing the short-term prospects for the market as a whole and then taking into account the impact of competitive variables. In the short run, factors such as ownership levels are likely to be less significant, while factors that may cause buyers to bring forward or defer purchases (such as changes in the cost of acquisition and use, buyer liquidity and weather fluctuations) will be more important. Income levels will be important, although the possible transitoriness of income changes needs to be taken into account.

Of these variables, most are relatively forecastable, although there may be problems with liquidity and elements of the cost of acquisition and use that are affected by government policy. Competitive policies that have a market-wide effect are likely to be forecastable from current trends (for instance a broadening of distribution network).

The analysis of the effect of competitive variables will probably require analysis of buyers' demand for different characteristics in products and of the extent to which the characteristics of the product/marketing mix provided by firms meets this demand.[2] Such a procedure is very demanding of survey data and is difficult to use for long-term analysis because of problems of data stability. However, it provides a firm foundation for the short-term analysis of demand.

Buyers have various characteristics in mind when they consider the purchase of a product. In this example, the characteristics might include efficiency of temperature control, power consumption, appearance, purchase price, noise level, availability from a particular distributor or kind of distributor, service network for the product and image associated with the use of the product. The success or failure of a particular product in market share terms can be explained in terms of the proportion of potential buyers for whom the product represents the best combination of characteristics. For each product, each buyer may have a different set of preferred characteristics, while the relative importance of each of these characteristics will differ among buyers.

There are two main ways of determining the buyers' trade-off among characteristics: interview and actual choice analysis. In cases where the product is new or infrequently purchased, there are problems in accumulating enough choice information and in obtaining information on preferences when the buyer has limited experience of the product. If this is so, it may be possible to obtain the required information by putting potential buyers in a simulated purchasing situation. Where buyers have enough experience of the product, it may be best to use questionnaire-based techniques to establish the relative importance of the characteristics and use the information so obtained in analysing actual choices.[3]

ACP might start its analysis by attempting to segment the market according to established preferences. For example, one group of potential buyers may hold low price and low power consumption for a given temperature control capability to be important, while another may hold low noise level, appearance, availability from particular distributors and reputation for reliability to be important. The next step would be to establish how each of ACP's and ACP's competitors' products performs on the basis of each preference cluster and to establish how this performance was related to market share. If segmentation of buyers according to preferred product characteristics can in some way be correlated with more general variables (such as income levels, social class, location, size of dwelling), then this would help both in orienting marketing policy and in predicting the evolution of demand.

The above analysis should also enable competitive policies to be taken into account. Changing prices, product designs, promotional and distributional policies affect each product's chance of succeeding in each market segment. Because ACP is concerned about the threat of increased Japanese competition, the appropriate point to examine is the likelihood of this competition being able to target its products more successfully than ACP. In addition, ACP will need to consider the effects of interaction between its policies and those of the competition. This will require the use of information about costs, aims and other internal aspects of competitors. For example, the demand analysis may show that despite the fact that split units are currently being sold mainly to the higher income groups, there is a substantial group of medium income earners who would enter the market if unit prices can be reduced by about 15 per cent. ACP would need to estimate the likelihood of Japanese competitors being able to reduce their prices so substantially in the short period. This depends on their production and cost conditions.

A more straightforward approach to the problem would have been to try to establish the correlation between market shares and marketing variables, without undertaking any analysis of characteristics demand. The outcome of such an analysis would be an equation relating ACP's market share to its relative price, its relative importance as an advertiser, relative size of its distribution network and some index of product quality.[4]

EXAMPLE 2: NEP LTD

Northern Engineering Products is a UK manufacturer of a range of machine tools. One of its divisions produces tungsten carbide cutting tools. Like most of its competitors, it produces a range of products, from brazed-tip tools to throw-away tips and tool holders; most of the designs are according to international standards. There is competition in price, availability from stock and quality of the tungsten carbide tip. Recent technical developments (the coating of the tungsten carbide tip with microscopic layers of other tungsten and titanium compounds) have considerably improved the quality of cutting materials but have made it difficult for the smaller firms to keep pace. This has left them with the choice of spending more on research and development in an attempt to match the product quality of the major producers – buying coating technology, farming out coating to firms with the appropriate knowledge, leaving the premium segments of the market to the major producers – or opting out of the product area altogether. NEP's problem is to assess the viability, over the next few years, of its position as one of the smaller producers, and in particular to investigate the feasibility of staying in the market by servicing only smaller buyer accounts. In order to do this, it needs to forecast the size of UK market over the next ten years, the likely market shares of the major producers (on different policy assumptions) and the size of the small accounts sector and its responsiveness to marketing policies that NEP might adopt.

For the long-term forecast, several general factors need to be taken into account. The first is the growth of the overall market for metal cutting tools , which is dependent on the state of the customer industry, the use of other metal forming techniques and the substitution of other materials for metal. The second is the development of substitutes for tungsten carbide (for instance diamond and ceramic materials).

The engineering industry produces goods which are subject to strong and prolonged cycles in demand. This may make it difficult to assess the long-term trend. However, certain general tendencies can be isolated. As far as capital equipment demand is concerned, some increase in the machine intensity of the economy can be expected over the long term. On the consumer durables side, because most durables are nowhere near saturation level in the UK, demand can be expected to grow faster than income. However, the substitution of electronic for mechanical and electro-mechanical controls may reduce the demand for precision-machined parts for many products. Design improvements can be expected to reduce the bulk of many products and hence their need for metal forming of any kind. Also, improved powder metallurgy techniques can be expected to increase the substitutability for machined parts of parts produced by powder metallurgy processes.

The impact of substitutes for tungsten carbide depends on relative prices and technological developments of their production and use. These result in changes in total use cost and in greater applicability of particular substitutes. Relative prices will also be affected by raw material prices. Tungsten supplies are concentrated in a few countries, while many tungsten compounds are used in defence industries. Unstable political conditions may therefore affect the price from either the demand or the supply side, or both. The raw material price is high relative to ceramic materials, and there is also the prospect of cutting tools being developed from silicon compounds, which have a very low material cost.

Taking into account factors such as the above involves technological forecasting.[5] Technology develops through the application of scientific discoveries.[6] The nature and timing of this process varies from industry to industry and country to country. In the tungsten carbide industry, whatever the source of discoveries, the process of diffusion into production and use tends to be carried out by the larger firms. However, given that the cycle of discovery, testing, production and market penetration takes at least ten years for significant innovations, major changes in the medium term should be predictable from current market opportunities and research findings.

Changes in demand resulting from technological developments may be analysed in the following way. First, identification of key competitive materials and key areas of application (where these materials have the greatest advantage) must be carried out. Then some estimate would need to be made of the likelihood of competitive materials being improved so that they can substitute more effectively for tungsten carbide. This will depend upon what discoveries have been made to date, what work is currently being carried out, what scientists think of the prospects of carrying the work further, what firms are involved in the work, how strong is their competitive position and how good they have been in the past at devising use-technologies for new products.

At the same time, tungsten carbide will continue to be substituted for other metal cutting materials, as part of its own process of diffusion.[7] An element of traditionalism in the UK engineering industry accounts for some work being carried out with high speed steel tools which could be better done with tungsten carbide tools. Also, there are jobs which – as currently designed or as currently executed (namely, with what machinery) – need high speed steel tools, although they could be done more efficiently if the job were redesigned or if newer, more stable machinery were used. As old machinery is replaced, the market for tungsten carbide cutting tools grows. Estimates of the growth of this market segment may be based on a study of the age distribution and character of machine tools currently in use.

The threat from import competition appears both in the tungsten carbide industry and in the industry's customer industries. Relatively low productivity growth in the UK engineering industry has led to its losing some of its market and to some degree of specialisation in low value per unit weight machines (suggesting less precision machining). This reduces the growth rate of NEP's domestic market. The threat from import competition in carbide products themselves is less serious because the major international firms have plants in the UK from which they supply most of the UK market. Any major market share change is likely to come from this source.

From the above, we can select the following variables for inclusion in the long-run demand analysis for tungsten carbide cutting tools in the UK:

National income (trend and fluctuations)
Investment goods demand
Demand for consumer durables
Technical change (perhaps measurable by tonnage of metal formed
    by different processes and by relative usage of, for example, metals
    and plastics)
Stock and age distribution of machine tools
Relative prices of tungsten and competing materials

The composition of overall demand will affect the viability of NEP's proposed strategy of servicing small accounts. The first step in the analysis is to establish the characteristics required by users. Here, a survey would need to be used to establish how different segments of the market trade-off the factors of price, service and product quality. The survey needs to be designed to test NEP's hypothesis that there is a large group of small customers whose major concern is not (like that of the large mass-producing engineering firms) to have the latest innovations in coated tips together with a very wide range of standard tips available ex-stock, but rather to buy a limited range of standard tips of known reliability at low prices. The analysis needs to be set up broadly enough to cover the market shares of the major producers, because if they are not able to supply the premium market, they may turn to the budget market in which NEP is interested. Because the major producers are involved in competition on a world scale, with presence in any given market maintained not necessarily for profitability but rather as a potential base for retaliation if their other markets are disturbed, one of the major producers may attempt to capture the small buyer segment (even though his distribution system, product range and technological policy is more suited to supplying the large buyers) because it would help to maintain his position in the market.

From the above, we can derive that the following factors should be included in the analysis of demand response to particular competitive strategies:

Size distribution of buyers
Buyer characteristics (kind of production process, organisation, etc.)
Pattern of demand for product characteristics (price, quality, range,
    service, etc.)
Supply by competitors of product characteristic combinations

ANALYSING DEMAND FOR PRODUCTS: STAGES OF THE PROCESS

Having considered two examples in detail, we can now suggest the general stages that demand analysis involves. Whether a particular stage needs to be carried depends on the particular policy options that the firm is considering. We divide the analysis into the long run and the short run without specifying the time periods to which these terms refer, since what is considered to be a short or long run by a particular industry depends upon the product and production system. The analysis is also divided into product group and product, again to be interpreted in a relative sense.

PRODUCT GROUP, LONG RUN

This is used to analyse the relationship between the development of the economy over the long run and the demand for the product group. It includes establishing the relationship between demand for the product group and the following factors:

1. *Per capita national income* (the effects of growth in personal disposable income and the extent to which rising income takes consumers through threshold and saturation levels of consumption of the product; if the good is an industrial good, the extent to which it is affected by trends in consumer goods production; effect of changes in consumption and production technologies caused by rising real price of labour implied by per capita income growth)

2. *Structure of the population* – size, age distribution, race, urbanisation, etc. (the effects on product demand of the age of user, personal life-cycle patterns of demand, urban – rural distribution of population, emergence of groups with special consumption habits, public expenditure associated with dominance of particular age-groups, with rate of urbanisation, etc.; effects of changes in patterns of communication caused by changes in the above variables)

3. *Changes in the industrial structure of the country* (effects of international competition, changes in relative prices of inputs, changes in capital structure of industry, changes in the regional distribution of economic activity and effects of changes in the concentration of industry)

4. *Changes in technologies of production and use* (switches in demand between product groups as a result of changes in relative performance;

extension of needs that are satisfiable by given product groups; changes enabling previously unsatisfiable needs to be satisfied; effects of government intervention to encourage the development of particular kinds of technologies)

5. *Changes in basic preference patterns of buyers* (fashion influences; effects of evolution of social concensus about what is desirable; influence of media; effects of producers' attempts to change preference patterns; changing receptiveness to innovations; effect of accumulated experience)

6. *Changes in distribution system for different product groups* (effects of availability of different product groups; conditions of availability; convenience of purchasing, etc.)

7. *Relative prices and total user costs of competing product groups* (effect of competition among product groups for buyers' budget)

8. *Prices and total user cost of products complementary to the group* (effect through buyers' budget)

9. *Input prices* (for product group itself and complementary and substitute product groups, for these explain relative prices)

10. *Ownership levels of product group* (important over the long term for long-life durables in explaining replacement purchases and approach to saturation levels)

11. *Stock or usage of complementary product groups*

12. *Financial factors* (effects of long-run trends in availability of credit to different groups of buyers)

13. *Government influences* (trends in government purchasing; standards legislation; taxation; subsidising, etc. and their effects on the product group)

PRODUCT GROUP, SHORT RUN

This is used to analyse the relationship between the short-run behaviour of the economy and the demand for the product group. It involves establishing the relationship between demand for the product group and the following factors:

1. *National income* (the effects of short-run fluctuations in national income on its components and on intermediate goods demand as analysed by input—output methods)

2. *Consumption expenditure* (effects of permanent and transitory

income perceptions; accumulation or running down of liquidity; changes in consumer finance, etc.)

3. *Fixed investment expenditure* (effects of past levels of investment, actual and expected returns to investment, cost of capital, output expectations, depreciation of existing stock, etc.; effects on consumers employed in investment goods industries)

4. *Inventory investment* (effects of running down or building up of inventories by customer firms; influence of expectations)

5. *International trade* (effects of imports on product group market; changes in relative prices; exchange rate changes; changes in government trade policy; effect of changes in export demand on product group)

6. *Government fiscal and monetary policy* (both as it affects national income and as it affects the product group in particular through specific commodity taxation, finance controls, etc.)

7. *Conditions of supply of substitutes and complements* (prices, availability, short-term impact of changes in product and process technology etc.)

PRODUCT, LONG RUN

This is used to analyse the relationship between demand for the product (given product group demand) and developments within the market served by the product group. It includes analysing the relationship between the demand for the company's product and the following factors:

1. *Competitive structure of the industry* (the effects of changes in the concentration of the industry, changes in barriers to entry caused by advertising, economies of scale, research and development, etc.; effects of changes in market share of imports; effects of involvement of firms from other industries; changes in structure of distribution for products in the competing group; changes in the relative productivity of competing firms; evolution of competitive strategy of each competing firm – balance among pricing, new product development, promotion and distribution)

2. *Production technologies* (effects of production process changes on marketability, costs, performance, etc.)

3. *Technologies of product design and of use* (effects of technological change on the way in which competing products are designed and used; effects on marketability, cost, reliability, etc.)

4. *Buyer characteristics* (effects of changes in the nature of the buying population on demand for competing products)

5. *Characteristics demanded by buyers* (effects of changes in buyer preferences among products in the competing group, acceptability of newness; relation between characteristics demanded in products and characteristics of buyers)

PRODUCT, SHORT RUN

This is used to analyse the relationship between short run market behaviour and demand for the firm's product. It involves analysis of the relationship between demand for the firm's product and the following factors:

1. *Own and competitors' prices* (effects of total user cost, discounts, price discrimination, finance offered with product, price awareness in different customer groups, etc.)

2. *Own and competitors' promotional policies* (effects of different methods of promotion, different advertising messages, use of different media, use of different sales force tactics, different sizes of budget for each activity, etc.)

3. *Own and competitors' distribution policies* (effects of location and type of outlet, discounts to distributors, etc.)

4. *Own and competitors' product line policies* (effects of product line modifications to suit products to buyer preferences, associated changes in marketing policies, etc.)

5. *Short-run changes in buyer characteristics and preference patterns* (effects of marketing policies; effects of recent experience with products; sampling behaviour; patterns of loyalty; changes in buyers' budgets and effect on trading up, etc.)

APPLYING DEMAND ANALYSIS

Once the basic dimensions of demand analysis have been set up, the next step is to quantify the analysis. In Chapter 7, we consider some of the more important aspects of quantification. Application in particular policy areas is discussed from Chapters 8 onwards.

6 Cost Analysis

For the marketing manager an important informational input into his decision making process is that concerning his firm's efficiency in using resources, in particular what it costs his firm to produce particular products and market them in particular ways. It helps if marketing management is able to assess independently the cost information supplied by accountants as data on which to base those marketing decisions. Let us consider an example to show how understanding cost analysis can improve marketing performance.

The marketing manager of HK Airmotors Inc., a US manufacturer of small air-driven motors, is considering an enquiry from one of his Middle Eastern customers. The enquiry could lead to a substantial annual order which would increase his unit turnover by 20 per cent. The net price at which this order might be obtained is his current full cost break-even price (calculated as an average over the different types of product involved in the possible order). He requests a recalculation of costs based on the estimated larger output from the company cost accountant; the only change the estimate shows is a reallocation of overheads over the new quantity of output. Because overheads are 20 per cent of total costs, their reallocation will reduce full cost by $3\frac{1}{3}$ per cent. As HK operates on a normal profit margin of 10 per cent of net price (estimated to be sufficient to meet its rate of return on capital aim), the deal will be difficult to justify. However, if the order is received at the current break-even price, and if overheads remain the same, profit margin will increase.

Suppose that at the moment, HK is selling x units at an average net price p. Since total cost is $.9px$ (90 per cent of revenue px), fixed costs must be $.18px$ (20 per cent of total cost). Variable costs are then $.72p$ per unit. The new order will increase production by $.2x$ units at a cost of $.144px$ (quantity of increased production multiplied by variable cost). Total cost will be $1.044px$ (old full cost plus cost of new order). The revenue from the new order will be $.18px$ (a 20 per cent increase of output at a price equal to old full cost), and total revenue will be

1.18 px. Profit is now 11.53 per cent of sales. The increase is due to the fact that reallocation of overheads (as the accountant calculated it) leads to a higher profit on sales other than those which come from the order in question, a point which is not taken into account in comparing the new full cost with the revenue from the new order. Note that overheads do not always remain fixed, nor do variable costs per unit always remain constant. For example, if the new order were to result in longer payment days and therefore a slower turnover of capital, it might not be advisable to accept it.

Cost calculations, as this example shows, affect even the most simple marketing decisions. In this chapter, we shall consider those aspects of economic cost analysis which are of particular importance in marketing decisions. There are two basic aspects of cost analysis. One is the definitional aspect (distinction between fixed and variable costs, marginal and average costs, the short and the long run, etc.). The other is the empirical aspect (why and to what extent do costs change as a result of particular policies).

DEFINITIONAL ASPECTS

The incremental or marginal cost approach is widely accepted as providing relevant information for management decisions. Briefly, instead of considering costs in terms of averages, analysis is in terms of changes in total costs produced by particular changes in policy. The marginal approach should be used with care in relation to overheads. Although a particular product or sales deal may be undertaken on a non-overhead bearing basis (that is to say, simply because marginal revenue exceeds marginal costs while not covering overheads as allocated by average costing procedures) and yield extra profit, it is worth asking what will happen when and if the product or sales deal becomes a major part of the firm's business (for example if existing products or markets have to be discarded).

There are two basic assumptions which lie behind this questioning of the advisability of 'marginal deals'. The first is that the firm has a limited resource base which should be used either to make as much profit as possible in the present or to develop profitable markets for the future. If resources are committed today to less profitable activities which absorb the resources for some time, then future profits may be forgone if other (more profitable) opportunities turn up and cannot be pursued because no resources are available.

There are circumstances in which this view is correct. If resources really are seriously limited, if there is no prospect of expanding them such that both future profitable activities and current contributors of marginal profits can be dealt with, and if the policies in question really do absorb these resources, then it may be appropriate to allocate the resources to ensuring future profitability. The economic interpretation of such a situation would be that the true opportunity costs of the resources have not been taken into account in the marginal cost calculation. If the resources really cannot be expanded, then their opportunity cost is the future profits that are forgone by applying them to present uses. It is important to check whether the resources in question can be expanded, as well as whether they really would be absorbed by the 'deal' in question. Returning to the HK example, it might have been argued that the manufacturing facilities that would be absorbed by the Middle East order could have been used more profitably by expanding sales in the US market. If this were true, then this would be an argument for expanding capacity, rather than conserving it for the home market. Each of the three possibilities (US expansion, export expansion, and US plus export expansion) needs to be evaluated for profitability.

The 'limited resources' argument against marginal deals may be used for marketing capacity. If it is difficult to obtain good sales and marketing personnel, then to use personnel up in doing marginal deals may waste scarce resources. It is therefore important to check how much of the firm's marketing and selling resources a particular deal or product absorbs, in particular how much servicing its customers require and may require in the future.

The second assumption lying behind questioning of the advisability of marginal deals is that overhead control may be inadequate. Firstly, servicing the deal may require more resources than were estimated at the time the deal was made. Secondly, the firm's activities may become more oriented towards deals which were originally marginal.

Increased absorption of overheads is only important if capacity in overhead services is fully employed. If this is the case, then using true opportunity costs in the marginal analysis may result in the deal being abandoned. The deal may only use *some* fully employed overhead services, so it may be worth while expanding these services to permit a deal which exploits other overhead capacities which are under-used. Points such as this may be anticipated if a serious attempt is made to break down overhead use by products or markets rather than averaging out total overhead use.

Reallocation of the firm's activities towards originally marginal deals may reflect a lack of direction in policy making and control at the highest levels in the firm. A marginal sales deal which is high in volume and low in profitability may absorb more and more of marketing management's attention at the cost of neglect of product and market development in the most profitable areas of the firm's activity. For this reason, it is important to keep a check on the contribution to overheads of different markets and products (related to scarce resource use). At the same time, it is important to realise that marginal deals may make an important contribution to the spreading of risk or the realisation of economies of scale (points that cannot normally be taken into account in simple contribution-to-overhead analysis, because they are based on interaction effects between markets or products).

THE SHORT AND THE LONG RUN

Some arguments about the real costs of particular marketing policies hinge on the difference between the short and the long-run situations. In the short run, for example, a marginal deal may put no pressure on resources. But growth in the other activities of the firm may mean that resources for which a marginal deal created employment come under pressure. For this reason, it is important to undertake cost analyses both for the short and the long run, using discounted cash flow techniques to reduce future figures to a basis comparable with present figures. Such analyses may show policies to be viable in the short but not in the long run, or vice versa. Here, it may be appropriate to undertake such policies on a strictly temporary basis, although there may be conflict between the need to exploit capacity to the full and the need to maintain customer goodwill by maintaining commitments.

EMPIRICAL ASPECTS

Because the appropriate input into marketing decisions is information concerning the extent to which total costs change as a result of those decisions, there may be problems in obtaining the appropriate information from the firm's costing system. This is because costing systems are designed partially to give a picture on individual costs which is consistent with some overall cost picture. In particular, the need for every cost to be allocated may lead to averaging systems being used to allocate overhead and also lead to historical instead of opportunity costs being used to represent resource costs (a particular problem with inventory usage).

There is no simple way of solving these problems, for the cost information system is an integral part of the control mechanism of the firm. To make exceptions to the rules governing the whole system may be justifiable on management decision grounds, but can lead to the undermining of the whole system and subsequent loss of management control. The ideal solution is to design a management accounting system for providing the opportunity costs of decisions together with average costs (for checking consistency of decisions with overall cost covering objectives).

If we can assume that appropriate cost information is obtainable, then the focus switches to how costs actually change with different policy decisions. The standard economic analysis of costs uses the notion of a production function for each product. A production function summarises what combination of physical inputs (time required from various machines, hours of different kinds of labour, materials, etc.) is required to produce a physical quantity of a product. The relationship depends upon the production technique used, the efficiency with which the inputs are used (for example whether particular inputs are being inappropriately handled or whether there is spare capacity in any input), the quality of the inputs and the scale of production. The cost function is derived from the production function by substituting the opportunity costs of each input for the input units.

PRODUCTION TECHNIQUES

Marketing requirements affect production techniques through product design and through the rate of production required. The extent to which the needs of small groups of customers have to be met affects the feasibility of high volume production. In particular, the trade off between variety of products and economies of scale depends upon the willingness with which customers requiring low volume items will pay.[1] Because commitments to particular production modes usually have to be made well in advance, one of the tasks of marketing management is to establish for how long the demand trends which seem to justify departure from existing modes of production are likely to last. Once production modes are fixed, then appropriate organisations tend to evolve.[2] This makes changing modes particularly difficult.

At a less general level, marketing management needs to consider the possibilities that advances in production technology open up for marketing policy (e.g. price reductions following the introduction of more efficient production techniques, product line changes following innovations). It is important to extend analyses of buyer behaviour to include price reductions or design possibilities which are *likely* to become feasible following technological change.

EFFICIENCY OF INPUT USE

One way in which marketing management can contribute to the efficiency of input use is, as we have seen, to identify situations in which spare capacity can be exploited. Another contribution that marketing management may make is to help exploit opportunities to reduce costs by learning from experience. Learning, whether on the production line, in the office or in the boardroom, is partly dependent on repetition of activities (although these do not necessarily have to be exactly identical).[3] Frequent model changes reduce the amount of learning that can take place about the production and marketing characteristics of particular products. Frequent changes of target market can reduce marketing learning.

In certain industries, experience effects may be well enough established for marketing policies to be based upon them. If learning is expected to result in substantial production cost reductions and is dependent on cumulative production, then it may pay to set initially a loss-making price for a new product in order to capture the market, on the assumption that learning will turn the price into a profitable one later on.

If experience effects are to be used as the basis of marketing strategy, it is important to establish their causes and effects. Experience effects have their origin in the following factors:

Increased labour efficiency There is evidence that manufacturing operations with similar labour content show similar experience effects.[4] As workers repeat particular production tasks, they find ways of improving their work, taking short cuts, and so on. The size of the learning effect also depends upon the proportion of production work that is worker-paced (that is to say, where the workers, individually or in groups, can speed up production operations). This also applies to supervisory and maintenance labour. The gains from labour learning depend on factors such as the quality and stability of the labour force, payment schemes which do not award all the productivity gains to the firm (in which case labour is unlikely to agree to work at higher productivity levels) or to the worker (in which case the firm does not benefit from learning),[5] and on structures of work organisation which increase the scope for the application of learning (for instance the use of self-managing work teams).[6]

Method improvements and process innovations Improvements in production technology can make substantial contributions to increased productivity. This may require devoting substantial R and D effort to investigation of production systems.[7] Marketing technologies can also be improved with experience, as marketing management learns how to suit policies to objectives.

Improvements in input costs, quality and mix To the extent that the firm uses manufactured inputs which are designed specifically for the firm's product or which are for other reasons subject to productivity gains as the firm's production accumulates, input costs may fall. Input quality may also improve, leading to a reduction in quality control problems. Management also learns to substitute cheaper inputs or to change the input mix completely to achieve a lower total cost.[8] Marketing management learns which marketing inputs are effective in achieving targets in particular markets.

Planning of activities and learning about the capacities of inputs Work is planned in the light of what is known about the capacities of the people, equipment and materials with which the work is carried out. With experience, managers learn about the capacities of the people working under them and the machines, plant, etc., with which they work. In the case of machines, it may be possible to work well in excess of rated capacity (which may be understated by manufacturers for protective reasons). This learning allows work to be replanned so as to exploit capacities more effectively.

Product modifications As experience with a product accumulates, its design may be modified to save material, allow more efficient manufacture, etc. Such changes involve marketing decisions. If marketing management has a clear understanding of production and input conditions, they may be able to initiate such changes. Standardisation of products is a special case of this. The best policy may be to seek ways of standardising (for example through components) which allow differentiation policies to be continued.

QUALITY OF INPUTS

Marketing policy can affect input quality through the learning process, but marketing management's main concern is with direct inputs into the marketing process. It is important for marketing management to move away from evaluating marketing inputs in budgetary terms. For inputs such as promotion, it is important to consider non-budgetary aspects first. The initial question should be not 'How much should be spent on promotion?', but 'What are the promotional objectives?'. This should be followed by an analysis of what means are available to achieve the objectives and what these may cost. Only in this way can marketing management achieve proper control of input quality.

SCALE OF PRODUCTION

Economies of scale have an important influence on the structure of industry, pricing and other aspects of competitive behaviour. As with spare capacity and experience effects (both sources of economies of scale themselves), the challenge to marketing management is to exploit any economies of scale that may be available, given buyer needs. Economies of scale are defined as reductions in unit costs as the scale of an activity increases. There are several dimensions of scale.

Total output of a particular product through time Apart from enabling learning to take place, this spreads the depreciation of assets specific to the product over a larger output. One marketing asset which is often highly specific is past promotional effort and goodwill. Exploiting this asset may require the marketing of similar products, the extension of the life of products, and so on.

Duration of production run and rate of production per unit time For a given market life and for given total sales over a product's life, there will be various ways of scheduling production. The longer the life and the higher the rate of production in each time period, the more economically production can be scheduled. Various forces are at work here, including the reduction of repeated set-ups, learning, the use of more capital-intensive processes of production (and associated ability to buy capital equipment which has higher capacity and is more specific to the job).

Standardisation of products An important role of marketing management is to investigate how far the firm's product range can use standardised sub-assemblies, either produced within the firm or produced to some wider specification outside the firm. This may be one of the most important contributions to productivity growth in the manufacturing industries and may allow service industries to achieve the same rate of productivity growth. In the latter case, the role of marketing in increasing customer acceptance of standardised services is particularly important.

Marketing economies of scale These depend on factors such as the size of sales to each customer, the number of customers in a given geographical area and the size of consignments to each customer. Marketing, like production, has set-up costs, learning effects, and so on. It may pay to concentrate on key markets or customers rather than diffusing marketing effort.[9] There may be a marketing threshold (a level of marketing involvement in a particular market below which it is completely uneconomical to operate).[10] However, this needs to be set against customers' willingness to pay for variety and the associated possibility of market saturation for particular products, implying strongly diminishing returns to marketing expenditure beyond a certain scale. Marketing economies of scale may also be available through control of markets, because increased firm size or market share can increase bargaining strength vis-a-vis customers or suppliers, which will in turn reduce costs, increase revenue and possibly reduce uncertainty (allowing more efficient production planning).

INPUT COSTS

The final factor affecting cost of output is the unit cost of inputs. Marketing decisions affect input costs through product design and standardisation. Also, accurate demand forecasting can help to increase the efficiency of production scheduling.

EMPIRICAL ESTIMATES OF PRODUCTION AND COST FUNCTIONS

To estimate the relationship between output and costs, a variety of techniques is available. For manufacturing cost functions, engineering data coupled with input costs may be used to produce an 'engineering cost function'. For a whole plant, this requires combining engineering data for a large number of processes. An alternative approach is to estimate production or cost functions statistically. A large number of empirical studies of costs have been carried out using regression techniques.[11] These tend to show that most products have constant marginal costs within the range of output studied, implying that once production is set up, extra units cost the same additional amounts to produce. Although theoretical analyses (for example to explain why industries are not dominated by one firm) have relied upon marginal costs rising over certain output levels (as a result of increased overtime payments, problems of work organisation at output levels close to capacity, etc.), this tendency seems to be outweighed by increased efficiency from other sources at higher levels of working. There is some evidence that as firms get very near to capacity working, marginal costs begin to rise, but such evidence is not completely reliable.[12] In the longer run, as firms adjust their plant size to cater for significantly different output levels, we should expect any rising marginal cost tendency to disappear, as the empirical evidence confirms.[13] However, if marketing factors are taken into account, there may be a tendency for the economies of scale generated by producing for a larger market to be outweighed by increased selling costs.

THE MARKETING MANAGER AND COST INFORMATION

The marketing manager plays a key role between the firm and its customers. He therefore needs to understand the process which enables him to supply the customer. The most significant information that he receives about this process is cost information. It is therefore important for him to be able to disentangle accounting costs from economic costs, to understand why costs move as they do and to examine the opportunities that are available for reducing costs through marketing policies.

7 Quantitative Aspects

We have postponed looking at the quantitative aspects of the previous three chapters until this chapter. Even in this chapter, there is relatively little figure work. This is the result of a conviction concerning the nature of marketing management's task. The marketing manager is not a figure processor, but a manager who has to make decisions on the basis of the information that he requests and receives. He does not have to be able to carry out the statistical procedures which are required to produce the information.[1] What he does need to be able to do is to present information so that it can be processed statistically, to interpret the results of the processing correctly and to structure his demands for information according to the feasibility of obtaining it through particular techniques. He needs to be familiar with the limitations of particular techniques. In sum, he needs to understand methodologies rather than methods. This will enable him to exploit the services of statisticians, computer scientists, market researchers and econometricians.

We start with the assumption that the situation about which more precise information is required has in some way been modelled. That is to say, the kinds of relationship that are expected to exist have been broadly defined. We also assume that information about the values of the variables included in the model is available. The task remaining is to establish the quantitative nature of the relationships in which we are interested.

GENERAL METHODOLOGY

Whatever the data being analysed, the technique being used to analyse it or the functional form of the relationship hypothesised, there are certain basic notions that are shared by most of the market research, econometric and statistical quantitative methods that are used in marketing. The most important notion is that of *sampling*. Only rarely can marketing management rely on obtaining information about *all* the potential buyers of his products, *all* the firm's production runs, etc. The data base from which he works is normally a sample of the population in which he is interested. If quantitative conclusions are based on sample observations, there must be criteria for assessing the reliability of inferences from the sample result. For example, sample information may show that a five per cent reduction in the price of a particular product produces a ten per cent increase in the quantity demanded, other things being equal. It is appropriate to ask what the range of demand responses (in the population) is from which this sample could have been drawn. The answer might be that there is a 95 per cent chance that the sample has been drawn from a population who would respond to a five per cent price reduction with an increase in demand of between eight and twelve per cent. Whatever is being measured (the proportion of a population with a given attribute, the slope of the relationship between two variables or the clustering of individuals by commonality of attributes) it is important to understand that the sample result only permits *inference* about the characteristics of the whole population. The narrowing of the inference range depends on sample size and (in some cases) on the degree of success in explaining sample variation (itself partly dependent on sample size). The greater the amount of unexplained variance, the less the confidence about population characteristics will be. In other words, the confidence intervals for, say, the coefficients relating explanatory variables to the variables to be explained will be wider the less successfully we have explained sample relationships. In general, before using statistical results, management should require significance tests to be carried out. Some of the newer statistical techniques used in market research (for example cluster analysis) may not have clear significance tests attached to them. Significance tests are based upon assumptions about the distribution of the variables being studied. One of the commonest assumptions is that the variables are normally distributed. If this assumption is invalid, then the significance tests (if based on normal distribution assumptions) are also invalid.

The more information that we try to extract from a given data base, the greater the problems with significance.[2] For this reason, it may be important for marketing management not to require analysis of too many variables (unless use of the results justifies a larger data collection budget).

If it is really essential to analyse the effects of more variables than the data allows, it may be possible to combine variables in such a way as to reduce the number that have to be handled at any one time. One method that can be used is that of canonical correlation.[3] If a set of variables $Y_1, \ldots, Y_n$ has to be related to a set of variables $X_1, \ldots, X_n$, then from each set of variables a pair of linear combinations can be constructed which have the maximum simple correlation with each other, and further pairs can be constructed (on condition that each variable so constructed has no correlation with a previously constructed variable). Alternative methods for reducing the number of variables are principal components analysis and factor analysis.[4] These are based on constructing new variables which are linear combinations of the original explanatory variables, with each new variable showing high within-variable correlation and being uncorrelated with other new variables. These methods are particularly useful in dealing with market research questionnaire results. Such questionnaires often cover a very wide range of topics, with respondents being asked to answer questions covering attitudes, purchasing patterns, socio-economic characteristics, and so on. The methodological hypothesis underlying factor analysis here is that there are underlying – but unspecified – factors at work, which account for the individual's response to the questionnaire and also, say, his buying behaviour. Factor analysis groups statistically related responses, but the meaning of a particular factor isolated in this way is partly a matter of judgement.[5] Because the factors selected normally leave some of the original data unexplained, the results of factor analysis should be used with care, usually only after other analysis has shown that the groupings have theoretical significance.[6]

The general principle illustrated by many quantitative methods in the marketing area is minimising the degree of misfit. In regression analysis, lines or planes are fitted so as to minimise the sum of squared deviations of observations from the line or plane.[7] The principle of discriminant analysis is that of minimising misclassification. The results of such procedures may be severely distorted by the presence of exceptional observations. Such observations should only be disregarded if they are truly exceptional, meaning that they are attributable to a disturbance factor which is unlikely to occur again, the inclusion in a sample of a really exceptional individual, and so on.

FUNCTIONAL FORM

The first practical step in quantifying a relationship is to decide in what form the variables involved in the relationship should be presented for analysis. Here, we need to take into account certain possibilities.

Multicovariation If the variables that we want to use to explain or forecast the variable in which we are interested are themselves related to each other, then we may have difficulty in isolating the separate effect of each of the determining variables. Any statistical relationship we try to establish is likely to assign weights to two intercorrelated determinant variables in a more or less arbitrary way. If we were to omit one of the two variables, this would not help, since the remaining variable would pick up the effects of both. If in the future the relationship between these two variables ceased to hold, then any prediction we might make using a relationship established by using only one variable would be likely to be inaccurate. The normal way out of problems of multicovariation is to try to find data or situations where there is no intercorrelation of determinant variables. For example, a covariation problem may be caused in a time-series study by two determinant variables having a time trend. Here, we should try to find cross-sectional evidence of the effects of the variables. Information obtained from such an analysis could then be pre-specified in a time-series analysis. However, cross-sectional analyses present problems of their own. These arise from the fact that cross-sectional analysis uses observations of the values of a variable from different individuals, markets, etc., instead of from the same individuals, markets, etc., over time. Because the ways in which, say, the behaviour of a given individual changes over time with respect to a particular variable differ from the ways in which behaviour differs between individuals with respect to that variable, cross-sectional and time-series analyses may produce different results. They will also probably involve the use of different explanatory variables.

Lagged relationships In some time series analyses, the value of the dependent variable depends on past values of the independent variables. For example, demand for capital equipment depends not just on this year's output level but also on that of past years. The permanent income hypothesis implies the dependence of current consumption demand on past levels of disposable income. However, unless the determinant variable in question fluctuates completely randomly, there will be some correlation between the different (yearly, monthly, etc.) values of the variable. This is another kind of multicovariation problem. Here we cannot resort to time-series analysis to solve the problem, for the problem has to be analysed using time-series data. One way out of this problem is to suppose that the effect of a given determinant variable bears a particular relationship to the effect of last time period's value of that variable. For example, we may suppose that the effect of last year's disposable income was a proportion b of the effect of this year's disposable income on consumption demand, while for the year before last's disposable income the proportion is b^2, and so on. If this notion is acceptable, then simple algebraic manipulation enables us to reformulate the problem so as to avoid collinearity of determinant variables.[8]

Dummy and proxy variables In considering which variables to incorporate into a relationship to be estimated, we have to take into account their quantifiability. However, quantifiability does not have to be interpreted in too narrow a sense. 'Qualitative variables' (e.g. comfort, style) are of particular importance in marketing demand analysis. If it can reasonably be supposed that there is a strongly polarised effect (for instance if a product has a particular characteristic, demand for it is significantly higher than if it does not), we can use a dummy variable, which takes the value 1 if the characteristic is possessed (in the above example) and 0 if it is not. The same procedure can be used for analysing demand over a period in which a certain kind of event (for example a war or a general strike) occurred, for only part of the period. The interpretation of the dummy is that it imparts a shift to the relationship. Dummy variables can be used to analyse situations in which the variable to be explained has a dichotomous value. In marketing, this allows us to analyse markets in terms of buyers and non-buyers. If we carry out a regression study of the effects of certain variables in determining whether individuals buy a product, and assign the value 1 to buyers and 0 to non-buyers, then the coefficients of the determinant variables can be applied to a particular individual's variable set to determine the probability that he will buy. Dummy variables can also be used to analyse the interaction effects of variables. For example, if we are analysing families to see how their purchasing behaviour is affected by their urban–rural location and their social class, knowing that families of particular social classes tend not to be randomly distributed between rural and urban areas, we could use one dummy for urban family, class A, one for urban, class B, and so on. Care must be taken in setting up the structure of a relationship in this way in order to avoid problems of multicovariation. In general, dummy variables represent a very flexible instrument for dealing with a wide range of quantification problems that occur in marketing. It needs to be recalled, however, that dichotomous variables of this kind may violate basic assumptions about the distribution of variables which form the basis of some statistical methods.

If the qualitative variable is not dichotomous, trichotomous etc., then we may be able to represent it by using a proxy variable. A proxy variable is a variable which replaces the one which we should like to use because we can find no way of representing the latter or because we cannot obtain information on it. For example, in analysing demand for a particular consumer durable, we might want to include a variable representing preference for holding assets in the form of consumer durables. Instead of using a questionnaire response, we might construct a variable consisting of the value of the individual's stock of durables divided by the floor area of his dwelling, on the hypothesis that as the individual gets better off, he tends to buy both more housing space and more durables, but a greater than average tendency to buy durables will be reflected in his having more durables per unit floor area. Such a proxy might avoid problems of correlation with income, the other major explanatory variable.

Simultaneity Often we are faced with a situation in which the relationship we want to quantify is two-directional. For example, sales are determined by advertising levels, but because advertising budgets tend to be related to past sales levels or budgeted sales, the relationship is two-directional. In this case, we are actually faced with estimating two separate relationships, namely, a sales equation and an advertising budget equation. The two equations should be solved algebraically to obtain two further equations (the reduced form) for the endogenous variables (those determined inside the model, in this case advertising and sales) in terms of the exogenous variables (those determined outside the model, such as price, income of buyer, etc.). This method raises problems concerning correlation between the error term (the unexplained part) and the explanatory variables. An alternative to the above method of indirect least squares is two-stage least squares, which involves regressing one of the endogenous variables on the appropriate exogenous variables, substituting the expression for the endogenous variable so obtained into the relationship for the other endogenous variable, and estimating this in turn. This method is only feasible where the original (structural) equations are identified. Without going into too much technical detail, identification refers to the way in which the exogenous variables occur in the structural relationships.[9]

Taking into account the above points, we can now consider the exact form of the function. In order to quantify a relationship, we need to hypothesise a particular kind of relationship between the variables we are interested in. At a basic level, this implies making a hypothesis about, say, whether the relationship between the dependent and independent variables is linear, curvilinear, log-linear, S-shaped, etc. We also need to hypothesise about the nature of causality. For example, we may hypothesise that the independent variables interact, in which case we may need to use principal components analysis or some other technique which allows us to group variables. The kind of use to which the information will be put will determine whether we want to use a straightforward estimating equation, discriminant analysis, probability functions, etc. The functional form used in practice may be a compromise between the theoretically desirable and the computationally practicable. A particular estimating technique is likely to be associated with the functional form.

Various kinds of relationship may exist between variables. Here we shall consider some of the basic types. The easiest to handle (both computationally and conceptually) is the simple linear relationship, which can be expressed in the form:

$$Y = b_0 + b_1 X_1 + b_2 X_2 + \ldots$$

Such a form implies that the effect of a given absolute change in an independent variable (the Xs) on the dependent variable (Y) does not depend on the original value of the dependent variable or on the values, any independent variable. The partial relationship between Y and each of the Xs can therefore be drawn in the form of a straight line graph. The effect of changes in other independent variables is simply to shift the relationship, as shown in Figure 7.1.

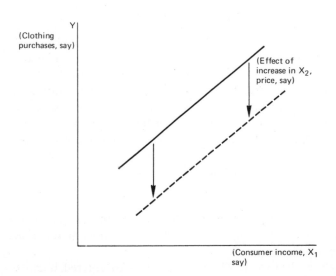

Fig. 7.1

In cases where we expect changes in independent variables to have a constant *proportionate* effect on the dependent variable, we can use a multiplicative form, as follows:

$$Y = b_0 X_1^{b_1} X_2^{b_2} \cdot \ldots$$

This relationship also has the computational convenience that it can be transformed into logarithmic form and then handled by straightforward linear regression techniques. The logarithmic form would be

$$\log Y = b_0 + b_1 \log X_1 + b_2 \log X_2 + \ldots$$

The coefficients b_1, b_2, etc. can be shown to be the outcome of a calculation to establish the relationship between proportionate changes in dependent and independent variables, or elasticity of one with respect to the other. Thus

$$b_1 = \frac{\text{Proportionate change in } Y}{\text{Corresponding proportionate change in } X_1}$$

Because we often find that the relationship between proportionate changes in dependent and independent variables is constant, this form is extremely widely used.

Some social and economic phenomena are characterised by relationships which need to be expressed in a more complex way. For example, investigation of the relationship between ownership levels of particular consumer durables and per capita income may show a threshold effect (once income rises above a certain level, ownership begins to increase rapidly relative to income) and a saturation effect (after income reaches a certain level, the rate of increase in ownership begins to level off). The diffusion of innovations through the population may show a similar relationship between the proportion of the population that have used the innovation and time. Although such relationships may be represented by more complex algebraic functions of the independent variable (e.g. $Y = a + bX - cX^d$ for a limited range of X), estimation may be rendered difficult by problems of transformation into a linear form or by multicollinearity. It may be possible to avoid such problems by using trigonometrical functions or functions of the exponent e.[10]

Whatever the form in which the variables are entered, it may be useful to set up the analysis in a probabilistic form, such that the equation estimated enables us to predict probabilities of particular events occurring. Instead of estimating a demand equation with the dependent variable being total amount demanded and the independent variables being average buyer income, price and so on, we may want to estimate the probability of particular individuals buying. This requires that the data be available on an individual basis. The outcome of such a procedure would be an equation in which the dependent variable was the probability of an individual purchasing and the independent variables were each individual's income, stock of the product, etc. Computationally, this can be handled by using a dummy variable for purchase/non-purchase. The interpretation of the equation is that it gives the conditional probability of purchase (conditional on particular values of income etc.).

Conditional probability equations are one way of analysing data in terms of a two-way classification. This can also be done with discriminant analysis, which can be used to explain the split of a population into several groups. The principle used is that of assigning weights to various attributes (e.g. income, price) so as to reduce the degree of misclassification to a minimum. Because standards of statistical significance exist for this method (as for the above methods), variables can be added to or dropped from the analysis according to whether their contribution to explaining the split is significant.[11]

Factor analysis is one statistical technique available for grouping observations according to the extent of their interrelation. An alternative approach (in some situations) is to use cluster analysis. Cluster analysis (there are several clustering techniques) can be used to answer questions such as 'How can consumers be arranged into groups such that within-group similarities in purchasing behaviour are as great as possible and between group similarities as small as possible?'. Because this is a relative question, answering it statistically involves hypothesising an absolute basis for comparison. An example is depicted in Figure 7.2 (overleaf). Suppose that we want to analyse the similarity of consumers in a particular group with respect to the frequency with which they make their food purchases and to their income. Each point represents the average position of a particular consumer over a year. One procedure for grouping the points would be to take the two points which are closest together, calculate their midpoint, and add to them the point which is nearest to that midpoint, proceeding until a specified number of points have been included in the cluster. The process is then repeated for the remaining points. Computer programs can be designed to allow points to be included in more than one cluster and to change cluster arrangements in an attempt to reduce the average within-cluster deviation from the cluster midpoint. Such a procedure is highly useful in market segmentation, although it raises problems with respect to significance criteria and fixing the limit to the number in each cluster.[12] Like factor analysis, cluster analysis can only be used for grouping rather than inferring relationships. However, it is a useful way of splitting up data before applying inferential procedures.

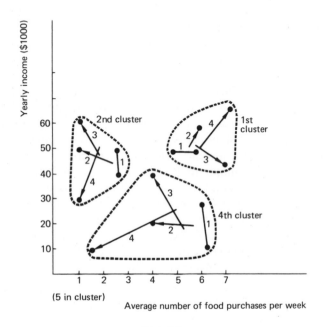

Fig. 7.2

QUANTIFICATION AND THE MARKETING MANAGER

In the above, we have tried to give some feeling for the different approaches used in quantification of relationships (whether demand, cost or industry structure), without going into details. As stressed at the beginning of this chapter, it is important for marketing management to take into account the significance of results obtained from such methods. Perhaps the best test of suitability is in use. If the methods used give reliable results, then this may be a better justification for their use than satisfaction of the most rigorous standards of statistical unbiasedness.

8 Product Policy

Product policy consists of a series of decisions taken on the basis of information derived from analysis of demand, costs and technical feasibility, taking into account business aims and strategy. Product line changes (except for minor line changes) normally have considerable strategic implications. They involve market, manufacturing and organisational commitment. We therefore need to consider both the strategic aspects of product policy and the more detailed aspects of individual product policy decisions.

PRODUCT STRATEGY

'Product strategy' can be defined as the framework within which particular product line changes are made. This framework includes research and development policy, organisational strategy, the corporate plan, and so on. A product strategy decision is one that gives a particular direction to product policies without implying that a particular product will be produced. The key economic aspects of product strategy are:

1. *Technological aspects* (R and D strategies, policies and achievements in the firm and the competing group of firms; the progress of scientific discovery and of the feasibility of different technological solutions to given product problems, etc.)

2. *Market aspects* (demand for particular kinds of characteristic in products; acceptance by market as measured by diffusion rate of new products; customer loyalty in the face of developing product advantages, etc.)

3. *Competitive·aspects* (general situation of competing firms; how their corporate, R and D and product strategies impinge on the firm's own product strategy, etc.)

1. TECHNOLOGICAL ASPECTS

Ability to exploit changes in process or product technology depends partly on the technological strategy followed by the firm. Ansoff suggests that there are various strategies that a firm might follow.[1] These are

First to market (implying a research intensive effort, supported by major development resources; close links between R and D and product planning; high proximity of firm's research to state of art; high R and D: turnover ratio; high product failure risk)

Follow the leader (implying development intensive technical effort; competence over broad range of relevant technologies; rapid response in product development and marketing; strong R and D–marketing–manufacturing linkage; high quality information on competitors)

Application engineering (implying high design and engineering skill but little R and D; ready access to product users; technically perceptive salesmen and sales engineers working closely with product designers; good product line control; cost consciousness; flair for standardising components)

Me-too (implying little or no R and D; strong manufacturing, dominating product design; strong price and delivery performance; ability to copy quickly and cheaply).

This gives some idea of the options that are open to the firm. This classification of strategies has implications for a series of inputs into policy (R and D, marketing and manufacturing effort). However, the connection between inputs and outputs is not straightforward. Let us consider the relationship between the inputs and outputs of R and D.

R and D inputs and outputs Assigning inputs into R and D costs raises problems. Measures typically used include R and D spending, R and D personnel levels and number of qualified scientists and engineers (QSEs). However, technological improvements can come from a number of sources other than those formally classified as related to research or development. Further, activities may be classified as related to R and D for reasons unrelated to the management of technical change.[2] Because there is some evidence that firms may base ideas about desirable levels of spending on R and D on industry averages, it may be important to take such points into account.

It is difficult to isolate the output of R and D such that the impact of R and D can be separated from other management variables. If the relationship between R and D spending and assets or sales growth is investigated, all kinds of extraneous influences are likely to be picked up (for example the influence of marketing policy or the reverse correlation between profits and R and D budgets). Variables that have been used to measure R and D output in a non-commercial way include patents awarded (or 'important' or 'significant' patents awarded) or important or significant inventions or innovations. Each of these measures has its own deficiencies. The patent recipient may not be responsible for the invention but only for its development (or not even this), while all patents are not of equal importance (a firm with a series of 'minor' patents may get a lower rate of return to R and D inputs than a firm which establishes one major patent). Further, some important innovations are not patented (seeking or achievement of a patent depends on administrative regulations and ease of circumvention). Despite these measurement problems, studies have shown that there is a strong link between most R and D input measures and most R and D output measures.[3] However, the strength of the relationship varies considerably in different industries, in different firms in the same industry and in firms and industries in different countries. The implication of this for analyses of Ansoff's type is that the characterisation of different kinds of strategy (for example particular R and D: turnover ratios) needs to be spelt out clearly in terms of the type of activity that is likely to be going on inside the firm (for example how much effort is likely to be devoted to basic research) and the outputs which that activity is likely to produce.

Technological strategy needs to be analysed in the context of the technological opportunities that are open. Technological change is related to the state of science, although the time lag is considerable.[4] Many studies of the effects of R and D inputs avoid this problem by studying firms within a competing group, for whom the technological opportunities available are more or less the same at any given time. However, a firm making a strategic choice among different kinds of activity chooses among areas where the technological opportunities are likely to differ. Differences in R and D inputs and outputs among industries are partially attributable to differing technological opportunities.[5] 'Technological opportunity' may not be directly related to scientific progress but rather to ease of achieving product differentiation, for a major incentive to high R and D involvement may be the gain that can be made by differentiating the product output of the R and D process from products produced by other firms. There is some evidence to show that in industries where product differentiability is high (consumer durables and investment goods), R and D levels are high.[6]

Although technological opportunity (in either sense) may provide the appropriate conditions for innovation, the innovative process itself may take place largely in response to technical problems or to basic economic incentives (for example whether overall demand in the product area is rising or static).[7] This and the above points have several implications for product strategy. First, marketing management needs to take into account the extent to which success in product strategy may depend upon the rate of progress in science and its successful translation into innovations. For example, if little scientific progress is being made in areas related to the firm's products (either in production processes or product design), high R and D activity levels may not produce the returns that emphasis on cost reduction, product standardisation and more efficient marketing may bring. Second, if the products of the firm are highly differentiable, emphasis on R and D may pay (depending on the nature of the product and on the stage of evolution of the market). Third, if demand for the product class that includes the firm's products is rising relatively quickly, then higher R and D activity levels are likely to pay, depending on the nature of market growth. If new product diffusion is rapid, firms which are second (or later) to market may be at a greater disadvantage than in markets where diffusion is slow, either because customers are slow to make a first purchase or because they take time to reach their full purchasing capacity.

The relationship between the inputs and outputs of the innovative process depends partly on how the firm is organised to handle it. Two factors are worth singling out for special attention: size of R and D organisation and of the firm carrying out the R and D and the nature of communication among the parties involved in the innovation. Both of these have implications for the organisational strategy of the firm.

As far as size is concerned, there is little evidence of economies of scale in R and D activity and some evidence of diseconomies. Larger firms seem to spend more on research per patent than do smaller firms,[8] and there is evidence that this does not reflect specialisation by larger firms in products that are difficult to develop or that are unpatentable, but rather the tendency of R and D projects to become more complicated by the process of bureaucratisation in larger firms.[9] It may be that better QSEs are attracted to smaller companies where they may be given greater latitude or at least may be able to influence the direction of development of the firm's R and D effort. More optimistic views on this point stress the complementary nature of the roles of large and small firms, with small firms concentrating on more specialised sectors and possibly making major advances in them, while larger firms concentrate on sectors where it is possible to apply advances in techniques to large-turnover products.[10] Major advances may often be made by smaller firms because at the time of the innovation there is no immediate application to large turnover markets. These points have two general implications for product strategy. First, if product strategy is directed towards achieving growth in the scale of the firm's operations, then this may affect the nature and efficiency of the firm's R and D operations. Firms relying on a 'first-to-market' or 'fast-second' strategy may need to take steps to maintain R and D productivity (such as organising R and D and associated marketing functions on a product basis and using less centralised management control systems, or acquiring small innovative firms, on condition that their innovative character can be preserved). Second, declining R and D productivity may result from concentration on projects with immediate high-volume applicability. Therefore, the consequences of concentrating on a few products or having a broad product range should be carefully considered. Although for a firm of given size, concentration on a limited product range will normally produce production and marketing economies of scale, it may have a detrimental effect on R and D productivity by reducing the range of activities in which R and D staff may become involved and by pressurising them to make small improvements to existing products instead of branching out in new directions. Product strategy should therefore take into account this trade-off between standardisation and R and D productivity. The 'state of the art' firm may be able to preserve R and D productivity by treating products initially as 'small firm products' and by making large-scale production and marketing arrangements only after R and D staff sever their direct connection with the product.

The contribution of R and D to commercial success depends on how it is integrated with the rest of the firm's activities. Studies confirm that R and D is not productive in isolation and that it needs to be in good two-way communication with other functions.[11] One major study suggested that successfully innovating firms encounter less opposition to the innovation on commercial grounds, seek the innovation more deliberately and make the decision to innovate more for marketing reasons.[12] The implications of these points are that R and D staff need to be in close touch with market needs, so that innovations are designed to offer a clear benefit to the user, that an innovation which arises out of a clearly defined marketing policy is more likely to succeed than one which arises in other ways, and that the whole process of innovation should be closely linked with the marketing process, with clear channels of communication between those responsible for initiating technical developments and the marketing staff. At the very least, marketing factors need to be introduced into the innovative process at an early stage. This implies a major role for sales force and market researchers as conveyers of information about user needs to R and D staff.

A related finding of the same study was that successfully innovating firms employ greater sales effort, devote more effort to educating users and give more publicity to the innovation than does the unsuccessful firm. This implies that innovations require a concerted marketing effort even if their technical appeal seems obvious to customers.

TECHNOLOGY STRATEGY RECONSIDERED

Firms do not have 'free choice' in their technology strategy. They are constrained not only by market and competitive factors, but also by a series of internal factors. A firm's capacity to deal with technological change depends on its size, the size of its R and D organisation, the distribution of responsibility within the firm and on the level of communication among different parts of the organisation and between the organisation and the outside world. Certain of these factors may be difficult to change without contradicting basic business aims. Given the need to adopt a particular technological strategy in order to implement a particular product strategy, the changes implied by the technological strategy may incur high costs. Disruption of established research, management and manufacturing procedures can produce control problems and dissatisfaction with jobs. However, the solution of changing slowly may not be available. A firm has either to be 'state of the art' or not; the difference between the two in organisational terms is immense. In addition, the competitive situation may not permit the firm to have the occasional lapses in performance that changing strategies may cause.

2. MARKET ASPECTS OF PRODUCT STRATEGY

Market factors that determine product strategy are of greater generality than those which determine product policy. In the case of product strategy, we are concerned with the general market conditions that affect the feasibility of broad lines of strategy, rather than with the particular conditions that make the success of particular products likely. The degree of success that a firm has with its product strategy is affected by its judgement of general market trends and its execution of policies based on that judgement. There is conceivably a situation in which an active product strategy (characterised by frequent product line changes) would have no scope. This would be in a market where every buyer's demand for characteristics in products was unchanging, where the number of buyers in the market was fixed, where their capacity to buy was fixed, where their information about the product alternatives available was perfect, where all firms were profit maximisers, where they all had perfect information about technologies and buyer demand, where all the resources and technologies required to supply any technically feasible product were available on the same terms to all firms, and where technologies were unchanging. In this situation, given that firms had had enough time to adjust to the situation, product strategy would be inactive. A given range of products would be in production, such that it yielded the most profit to firms. Each of the above assumptions precludes one source of product strategy. Let us consider these assumptions in turn.

Demand for product characteristics The demand for product characteristics is a result of a series of influences on the buyer. These influences include psychological factors, experiences, education, social background, occupation and income. As buyers become acquainted with new patterns of behaviour, (in particular purchasing behaviour) as they change their cultural level, occupation, and so on, so too will their demand for product characteristics change. We can separate these influences into those that relate to changes in buyers' personality and those that relate to changes in the influences to which they are subject. Personality-related influences are likely to operate more slowly on demand for product characteristics. Personality evolves slowly, as a result of various long-term factors. As a person's personality changes, so will the kind of characteristics he demands in products. Influence processes (which may also change personality) can operate very quickly. Contact with a group of people whose purchasing habits are significantly different can change the buyer's demand for characteristics through a rapid demonstration process. Whatever the speed of influence, the more the buyer is exposed to changes of the kind mentioned above, the more likely his pattern of preferences is to change, and the more likely he is to look for new ways of satisfying his needs. Differences among individuals in exposure to change lead to differences in their acceptance of new products, an important factor in explaining different rates of diffusion of new products.

Similar processes are at work in industrial markets. As the nature of a firm's research, production and marketing processes change, the behaviour of the firm as a buyer changes.

Number of buyers in the market As the number of buyers in a market grows (assuming each buyer's budget to be fixed), so the size of potential markets grows. It may become feasible (because of economies of scale) to produce products which were previously unprofitable.

Capacity to buy As an individual's capacity to buy (income and assets) grows, he is able to satisfy wants which were previously too expensive to satisfy. In industrial markets, as a firm's value added grows, so it requires additional inputs. In the short run, the kind of goods that a buyer buys may not change very much as his capacity to buy increases. Over the longer term, he is likely to change his pattern of behaviour more significantly, particularly if increased purchasing power is used to buy goods such as education, housing or leisure, which will change the whole framework within which the buyer consumes products. The scope for active product strategy is therefore greater in markets characterised by steadily rising incomes.

Product knowledge As long as buyers' information about which products are available remains incomplete, there will be scope for product strategy. Even though there may be products that exactly fit a buyer's requirements, so long as he is not well informed about them, there is an opportunity for other products to capture his demand.

Information about products reaches the buyer not just through the original supplier of the product but also through other buyers and users (hence the emphasis in new product diffusion theory on the processes of communication and influence[13]). Whether information is received, paid attention to and absorbed depends upon several factors: the characteristics of the buyer (how he absorbs information, what his priorities are in absorbing information, how long he gives attention to the information), the characteristics of the source of the information (advertising, friends and colleagues, experts, and their status and experience relative to the potential buyer), the characteristics of the message or information (how it is put over, in what detail, in what context, etc.). It also depends upon whether the buyer is in a position to receive information.

The factors discussed above are the main demand side factors affecting the feasibility of product strategies. In evaluating product strategies, management should take into account the extent to which success is dependent on these strategies. Different kinds of product strategy will require different mixes of market characteristics. For example, first-to-market strategies are more likely to succeed where diffusion is very rapid, while imitative strategies may fare better where diffusion is slow and where product information is not well diffused.

3 COMPETITIVE ASPECTS

Let us now consider the supply assumptions made earlier. Because the assumptions made with respect to the supply side are highly interdependent, we will consider them as a group. Because firms do not possess perfect information on technologies and buyer preferences, active product strategies may be feasible in situations in which preferences and technologies are constantly changing and where a firm can exploit its own position to obtain information more quickly than its competitors. Exploiting this information may enable the firm to build up a protective barrier round its markets, thus increasing the gains from product strategy. This tendency would be enhanced if the firm were able to create for itself a privileged position for obtaining resources needed for particular kinds of products. This raises the question as to whether there is any link between degree of monopolisation of an industry and innovativeness. One study of this topic concentrated on the 'truly' innovative aspects of product strategy by comparing a ranking of the extent of monopolisation of thirteen US industries (measured by ease of entry and market share of industry price leaders) with a ranking of their importance in innovation (measured by the number of patents issued, the number of scientists with doctorates and the presence or absence of a research department dealing with the development of new products or processes).[14] the two rankings were found to be uncorrelated; this suggests that although some degree of monopoly power may be necessary for technical progress, it is not sufficient.

In fact, finding a simple correlation between market structure and degree of innovativeness would be surprising. Monopolisation tends to be associated with larger firms, and we have already seen that the size of firm may adversely affect standard statistical measures of innovativeness. Further, degree of monopolisation may be related to production economies of scale and to the economics of large-scale marketing, neither of which bear any necessary relation to innovativeness. Indeed, firms which reap substantial economies of scale in production and marketing are precisely those which may suffer from problems of stifled innovativeness amongst R and D staff.

These points are reinforced by empirical studies that have been carried out on the relationship between industrial concentration and R and D effort.[15] In most studies, there is a suggestion of only weak correlation. One study suggested that evidence of a fairly strong correlation between concentration and research effort may be explained mostly by the correlation between concentration and technological type of industry.[16] One hypothesis concerning this connection is that technological innovation arising principally from technological opportunity leads to concentration because only a few firms succeed in exploiting this kind of opportunity. It may also be that the feasibility of maintaining a product lead by continual exploitation of new technology in contrast with product differentiation varies among industries. In any analysis of the influence of competitive variables on product strategy, we therefore need to take into account product differentiability.[17]

There· is some evidence that the effect of barriers to entry on innovative effort is rather complex. One study suggested that innovative effort may be highest when barriers to entry are moderate (rather than very high or very low), because when barriers to entry are very high, no major innovative effort is needed to succeed, while when they are very low, the fruits of innovative effort may be stolen very quickly from the innovating firm.[18] The notion of 'barriers to entry' may have a restricted significance in the case of 'true' innovations. The innovating firm in this case is less concerned about marketing–resource-based entry into its markets than with entry based on production or R and D resources. In analysing the relationship between R and D effort or output and barriers to entry, it is more appropriate to concentrate on this kind of barrier.[19]

In situations of competition among a few firms, rivalry in R and D may develop as a result of rivalry in product strategy or rivalry to reduce production costs. Rivalry in R and D may become an end in itself, with firms attempting to match R and D expenditures on the basis of available information. The hypothesis of similarity of levels of R and D spending between firms in concentrated industries has been tested and some evidence has been found to support it.[20] The implication of this point for marketing management is that it is important to ensure that R and D and marketing remain closely linked to prevent R and D advancing beyond market needs.

The success of a strategy for differentiating products may depend upon the extent to which research effort has to be diffused in order to achieve differentiation. Empirical studies of the effects of the dispersion of R and D effort over different products produce conflicting results; some imply that R and D is more effective if concentrated in a few product areas, while others imply that it is more effective if diffused.[21] There may well be pressures at work in both directions, with economies of concentrating effort being offset by reduction in productivity of R and D staff if they are obliged to work on projects which must show applicability to high volume products.

The feasibility of particular product strategies is also affected by the longer run dynamics of the competitive process, in which industry structure, buyer demand and technology interact. Schumpeter judges buyer demand to be highly dependent on producer activity in the long run (in the short run it is taken to be less dependent).[22] The producer is considered to be the engine of progress, pulling the buyer along with him rather than responding to changes in demand, attracted by the higher profits to be made by innovating. His ability to innovate depends on his ability to attract capital, but the profit he makes from innovating are eroded by imitations and more innovations. In general Schumpeter sees little stability in the competitive process. Realistically, we should expect this process to be modified by barriers to entry, and an enduring commitment to active product strategy to be sustainable in industries characterised by moderate barriers to entry.

The Schumpeterian process of 'creative destruction' of firms is similar to that envisaged by Downie, who hypothesises that differences in productive efficiency among firms are caused mainly by differences in the information inputs into those firms and are reflected mainly in higher profit accumulation rates in the more efficient firms.[23] The latter take business away from less efficient firms by being able to charge lower prices. They also have greater profits on which to draw for investment. This encourages less efficient firms to innovate to stay in business. The analysis can be extended to product innovations. New products produced by innovating firms may reduce absolute demand for other firms' products, leaving them with unused capacity, higher overheads and higher unit costs. The innovating firm becomes more efficient through its increased scale and through its investment in new and more efficient capital equipment to produce the new product. Firms which innovate successfully have less incentive to innovate again in the immediate future because they are not under pressure from low profits. Some confirmation for this kind of process can be found in statistics on the rise and fall of firms and their moves in relative profitability. The hypothesis is also supported by Mansfield's finding that a leader with one innovation is likely to be relatively slow with the next innovation.[24]

How far firms can compete by using product strategy depends partly on the managerial resources available to them. Penrose holds that managerial resources are the crucial determinants of a firm's rate of growth, because they dictate the firm's capacity to undertake policy change and (given the fact that management cannot be trained instantly) the rate of creation of additional management resources.[25] Firm's resources are not always fully exploited, and spare resources (as noted in Chapter 6) provide a challenge to the firm to find a use for them. There are limits to how far a firm can expand in existing markets and with its existing products by using up spare resources without a fall in profitability.[26] However, spare resources (including new spare resources created by indivisibilities in resources acquired in order to facilitate exploitation of the original spare resources) may be adaptable for use elsewhere. If a firm is to survive the pressures created by its competitors' desire to expand, then it will need to research new ways of using its resources. This will lead to competition in creativity among firms.

COMPETITIVE ASPECTS: IMPLICATIONS

Having considered a number of economic aspects of innovation and product competition, we can now sum up their implications for product strategy. Broadly, active product strategies will be more necessary or advantageous in the following circumstances:

1. the more difficult it is to obtain information about buyer wants and about technologies (the benefit to the firm that exploits information most effectively will be greater because imitation will be more difficult; active product strategy is likely to be more risky in these circumstances) and the better the position the individual firm is in to obtain such information (this depends parts on its market research, management and R and D resources and partly on its history of involvement in the market);

2. the greater product differentiability (this provides a means of defending gains in profitability that arise from innovation);

3. the greater the technological opportunities in the markets in which the firm is involved (this depends not just on the progress of science but also on the ability of industry in general to absorb the results of progress, because for the individual firm this determines whether there is a network of suppliers of components and materials needed for the firm's new products);

4. the more moderate (but not non-existent) the barriers to entry into the firm's markets (if they are very high, the risk of entry is low and a given innovation can be exploited for a long time and with great

profitability; there is therefore no need for a stream of new products, unless firms within the barriers follow a policy of intensive product development);

5. the more the competing group of firms is characterised by R and D rivalry (product strategy is only one of the ways in which R and D output may be exploited; cost reducing R and D efforts on the part of one firm may be met by new product oriented R and D efforts by other firms);

6. the easier it is to obtain finance for innovation (firms who most need to launch new products may be those in the least sound financial position; an unsophisticated capital market – one which is unable to appreciate the chances of success of an innovation and which reacts to uncertainty by the imposition of a very high risk premium – may make it difficult for a firm to recover once it has been worsted in the innovative race, unless it has other sources of profit; this suggests that diversification may help to ensure the continuing success of product strategy); and

7. the greater the firm's spare resources and the greater its market share for existing products (this dictates the relative profitability of putting the resources to use in the development and marketing of new products for new markets).

PRODUCT POLICY

Product policy decisions are investment decisions. They involve the absorption or release (in the case of product withdrawal) of resources. If a product policy decision can be expressed in cash flow terms (one flow corresponding to revenue and one flow corresponding to opportunity costs), then the decision may be made using discounted cash flow techniques (net present value, internal rate of return, etc.). In practice, information availability restrictions may require the use of other decision criteria (for example the 'fit' of the product to the firm's current resource base). Many of the information problems that occur in the context of product policy relate to demand. Product policy can be likened to 'shooting at a target' of consumer or buyer wants, with most of the information problems relating to the location of the target. However, as Abbott points out, the target is rather a complicated one, as are the 'scoring rules'.[27] Each buyer, given his basic preferences, can be assumed to have a series of want-clusters. Each want cluster is composed of a set of characteristics which the buyer desires in a product. The intensity with which the buyer desires each characteristic varies. For example, he may be highly particular about colour variations in a particular product but almost indifferent to price variations. The problem of the marketer is to make profit (or to achieve whatever business aim) by suiting his products to want-clusters.

Each buyer is willing to pay a certain amount for a product which exactly fits one of his want-clusters. As product characteristics depart from this exact fit, so willingness to pay may change. The buyer may be willing to trade off one characteristic against another, such that the relevant cluster may be a number of possible combinations rather than just one combination. The nearness of a product to an individual buyer's want-cluster is determined by the number of characteristics which are satisfied by the product and the weighting applied to them and to the unsatisfied characteristics. Characteristics demand may be interdependent; one characteristic may be demanded only if another is present, while the absence of one characteristic may make all other characteristics irrelevant. For the individual firm, the situation is complicated by the fact that other firms are likely to be shooting at the same targets. Scoring is therefore not absolute but relative to the other products on offer.

The feasibility of producing a commodity which achieves a high score with buyers and at the same time satisfies the firm's business aims is partly determined by the costs of building appropriate characteristics into products. There is unlikely to be a 'best' product for a given firm to market to a given set of buyers. A firm's business aims may be attainable by aiming either to be fairly close to a large number of want-clusters with a low price or to be very close to a small number of want-clusters with a higher priced product. A firm may be fortunate enough to be able to market a product which is closer than all other products to a large number of want-clusters, although in this case competitive pressures are likely to be intense. As want-clusters are mobile (changing with buyers' experience, learning about products, etc.), while the trade-off among characteristics included in clusters may also vary, there is likely to be room for a wide range of products in a given market.

To handle this situation empirically, market research analysts have developed a number of techniques to help in product positioning. These techniques involve factor analysis, discriminant analysis and clustering techniques for classifying and differentiating among groups of characteristics that are in demand, for differentiating between groups of customers to whom particular characteristics are of different importance, and for establishing trade-off rates for different product characteristics.[28] These techniques normally provide a better insight into the working of the processes that determine demand than analysis of demand at the level of products. The output of these techniques may be as precise as market share predictions for products embodying particular characteristics. These can be combined with more conventional economic demand forecasts (using regression techniques) for the whole market to produce sales volume forecasts. If the costs of producing the various combinations of characteristics (products) can be forecast for different levels of production, then manipulation of the price–volume–profit relationship may enable the firm to choose the products which best satisfy the firm's business aims. At this stage, interaction between promotional costs and returns will also need to be considered.

NORMATIVE APPROACHES

In practice, evaluating every combination of characteristics which has been identified by demand analysis is too expensive (in terms of information gathering and management information processing). Various rules or guidelines are used in product selection and these may help in evaluating the list of proposed product projects. This 'normative' approach has to be used with care, for no *a priori* set of rules can really cope with the variety and complexity of business situations encountered by different firms.

Product policy choices are not normally 'once and for all' choices. There are several stages of choice; each is accompanied by an editing process. At any one time there will be several product concepts under consideration by marketing, R and D and other departments. Selecting which concepts are suitable for further analysis, further market information gathering, further research or development or trial production is a process which is repeated until a final decision is taken to commit the firm to a full production run destined for the market. For firms which produce only to customer order, this part of the process of management is not so complex. But some mass production firms have to order parts and tooling a very long time in advance and may have to be fully committed some time before the product is launched. Whatever the degree of a firm's commitment to a particular product, it is important to keep product policy decisions under review until relatively late on in the process, in the light of new information or revised acceptance criteria.

Compatibility of resources One rule used to evaluate product concepts relates to the extent to which the product would use resources already possessed by the firm. This implies that the firm's comparative advantage lies in its existing activities and if comparative advantage were the sole decision criterion, diversification would be excluded. In practice, it is often used in conjunction with profitability forecasts as an indicator of the degree of risk that is likely with particular projects. To apply this rule, it is necessary to draw up an inventory of the firm's resources (personnel, management, equipment, etc.) and to rate them for their suitability for particular kinds of activity, relative to the resources possessed by firms with whom the firm may come into product competition. It is also essential to weight resources for their contribution to success. For example, a firm considering a particular product and wanting to evaluate its distribution resources for that product needs to consider the importance of distribution (relative to other resources) as a contributor to success in the market in question, how strong its own distributional resources are compared with those of its competitors and what demands the particular product makes on distributional resources. In its most sophisticated form, this rule involves the construction of an index of product compatibility, which is then used to rank different product projects. Because resources can be acquired according to the needs of particular products or product line policies, the approach should strictly take into account the ease and cost with which the appropriate resources can be acquired. If there are limits to the availability of resources, or if the firm's own resources are used to capacity, then this too should be taken into account.

Product gaps Used as a rule to isolate product concepts and to evaluate them preliminarily is the notion of 'product gap'. A gap is defined as a combination of characteristics (each of which is normally embodied in at least one product already on the market) which is not embodied as a combination in any one product. The existence of a gap may be evidence that no demand exists for the combination or that the combination cannot be produced at a marketable price. Appraisal of the significance of a gap must take into account technological possibilities, costs and competitive factors.

Risk At the earliest stages of product choice, it is difficult to attach probabilities to the chances of success of particular concepts. Forecasting techniques may yield probabilities for demand and cost figures, but if competitive reaction is involved, suggesting values for risk is difficult, even at the latest stages of evaluation. Subjective risk estimates may be used to evaluate concepts, with risk being minimised for a given expected profitability. Because profit is partly a reward for risk, making profits in some markets may involve particular risk levels. In such cases, it may be appropriate to take a portfolio approach to risk, accepting some riskier projects on condition that the desired overall risk portfolio of the firm is not too drastically disturbed. Because many firms have products which are affected similarly by the same states of nature, the sensitivity of the total product portfolio to changes in the business environment should be tested. The effect of new products on the portfolio may be tested by simulation (with and without the product). Note that riskiness can be reduced (at a cost) by purchasing more information or (where riskiness is related to uncertainty concerning successful development) by using parallel development strategies.[29]

Diversification or penetration The decision whether to concentrate on products which are of the same kind as or significantly different from the firm's existing products relates to exploitation of the firm's existing resource base as well as to risk. Most diversification tends to be 'concentric', involving an outward extension which exploits an existing technological or marketing base.[30] If a firm has growth in turnover or profits as its prime aim and is operating in markets where its ability to expand or increase profits is limited by competitive factors (such as the presence of well-entrenched competitors likely to react strongly to any attempt on its part to increase market share) or demand factors (such as small size of the market relative to the firm's existing sales level), diversification may be better pursued by acquisition. This applies particularly where the area of interest requires an accumulation of technical or marketing experience which cannot be acquired in a short time on the basis of internal expansion.

Various studies of patterns of diversification have been undertaken.[31] They are mostly based on industrial classification statistics and may therefore miss changes in product policy which from a marketing point of view would be considered to be diversification although they are moves within the same product grouping according to the statistical classification. Diversification tends to take place into industries which are younger, faster growing or with a higher rate of technical change. In newer industries, barriers to entry are likely to be lower, while the prospects for growth may be higher. There is a lack of general agreement in the empirical studies as to whether diversification achieves one of its aims of increasing the profitability of the firm,[32] although there is evidence that lower variability of profits is achieved.[33]

Product choice and marginal analysis As pointed out in Chapter 6, when marginal analysis is applied, account needs to be taken of changes that might occur over the long run which make policies which were undertaken on a marginal basis the main business of the firm. In the case of sales policies, the problem may be solvable by switching sales to more profitable markets (if they can be found). A product which is introduced on a marginal (non-overhead carrying) basis may not have markets where it can be marketed at a higher price. There are products which can *only* be supplied on a marginal basis. Demand simply may not justify the establishment of a production unit to cater solely for the demand for the product in question. An example of this is off-peak public transport in some large cities. In such cases, it is important never to get into a situation where the product has to bear the overhead.

Problems may arise with respect to the allocation of overheads which are associated with new product development, such as R and D costs. Companies with high R and D : sales ratios may take the view that R and D is such a large and fast depreciating asset that it is too risky to treat it other than as a current cost which is marginal to each product. However, this should not preclude products being undertaken on a marginal contribution basis, so long as their marginal costs are calculated to take into account true opportunity cost (including that of R and D).

DEMAND ANALYSIS FOR NEW PRODUCTS

The analysis of demand for new products can be divided into two parts: the analysis of the immediate reception of the product and the analysis of the diffusion of the product. Factors that influence the immediate reception of a product may differ from those that determine its long-term market performance. In the short term, there are special effects due to the newness of the product, the inability of buyers to adjust purchasing patterns immediately to include the new product, the inability of competitors to respond immediately, and so on. In the long run, the product becomes accepted as one of the range of products available, buyers adjust their purchasing patterns, competitors respond and social and commercial influence processes start to work for or against the product, according to whether its performance has met expectations, what kind of consumers are buying, what their influence is, and so on. At the same time, economic factors (such as incomes and prices of complementary and substitute goods) have time to change significantly enough to affect the demand for the product.

Forecasting the immediate reception of a new product involves extending methods discussed in this and the previous chapter. One procedure that may be used is 'concept testing',[34] which basically requires the use of a combination of statistical techniques to establish the relationship among characteristics embodied in products and sales levels. Because in some industries new product launches are accompanied by attempts to pull buyer preferences in the direction of the product, it is important to incorporate the results of tests of the effectiveness of persuasion into concept testing, perhaps by introducing some correction factor. In general techniques which are used several times in the same general market area can be substantially improved to allow for the effects of launch publicity, early working of the communication process, and distributional factors. For products which represent a complete departure from the firm's normal marketing context, concept testing is unlikely to be reliable.

If test marketing is an available option, then the main forecasting problems relate to the typicality of the test market and the influence of untypical events (particular supply problems, problems of persuading distributors to stock, changes in the economic environment and initial quality problems, for example). The length of time for which a product is test marketed (as well as the date of commencement of the test) must be chosen on the basis of likely repeat purchase patterns, expected purchasing cycles, competitor response time and changes in the economic environment.

The diffusion of innovation[35] is actually several diffusion processes taking place simultaneously. The classic stages of buyer awareness, interest, evaluation, trial and adoption[36] each produce their own diffusion process. These are affected by the diffusion of information, influence, marketing effectiveness, and so on. In the case of industrial products, the purchase of which may be a shared decision, there may be a persuasion and influence process that is internal to the firm. Here, key factors will include the management style of the firm and the riskiness of the purchase decision for the firm and decision makers involved. Attempts have been made to establish typical diffusion patterns in order to provide a tool for marketing management. The notion of the product life cycle embodies elements of the diffusion process (coupled with competitive and innovative processes). However, it is clear that there is no sufficiently general pattern in the sales performance of new products for marketing management to use the concept predictively.[37]

If a firm is willing to allocate enough resources to information gathering and processing, it may be able to build a predictive model for new product demand, as long as the new products are not so different from existing products that little relevant buyer behaviour data is available. Such a model would include econometric product group forecasts, product attribute ranking exercises, analysis of buyer demand for characteristics, estimates of competitive policies and estimates of the time it takes for the various diffusion processes to work. Repeat purchase forecasts would need to be included, as would forecasts of distribution availability. For the longer term, forecasts of saturation levels would need to be incorporated.

PRODUCT STRATEGY AND MARKET CHOICE

In this chapter, we have concentrated on product strategy and policy independent of market choice decisions. Market choice decisions are normally implicit in product decisions and may determine them. In the next chapter, we consider some economic aspects of market choice decisions.

9 Market Choice

Markets (which we define in this chapter as groups of buyers) can be classified for marketing decision purposes in various ways: geographically (national, regional, urban/rural), by income level, occupationally, by social class, by competitive basis (for example intensity of competition in market), behaviourally (for example people with certain leisure activities or buying habits), and so on. In industrial markets, classification may be on an industry basis (goods produced or technologies used), size of purchasing budget basis, ownership basis (public, communal or private), form of purchasing basis (tender, order, etc.), geographical basis, and so on. Markets may also be classified according to sensitivity to key variables (to price, free offers, etc.).

MARKET SEGMENTATION AND MARKET CHOICE

Two general reasons account for the need to classify buyers into different markets. They are that buyers have different *responses* to the variables that make up the marketing mix and have different *accessibility* to marketing policy. Put more basically, buyer groups are distinguished by how the firm gets to the buyer and by how the buyer responds. For marketing policy purposes, segmentation is most worthwhile if the firm can discriminate amongst segments in the application of policies. However, identifying a segment which does not currently permit discrimination may be an incentive to develop ways of isolating that segment. Attempts have been made to classify large groups of buyers using comprehensive classifications to indicate all kinds of modes of subdivision. These attempts, usually based on personality or sociological measures, tend to produce groupings that are too broad for marketing purposes.[1] Using situation-specific bases for classification of markets (for instance heavy and light users of a particular product, brand loyal or brand switching) may have some advantages over more general classifications, but raises other problems. For example, loyalty may be due to force of habit or to unwillingness to accept the risk of buying a different product, rather than to satisfaction with the product currently bought. The market behaviour implications of situation–specific classifications are therefore not always clear.[2] It may turn out that within a particular segment, there is no homogeneity of psycho-social characteristics or of response or accessibility to marketing policy.

Given the use of the multivariate techniques described in Chapter 7, we may not need to take too fixed an *a priori* view about the particular kinds of variables which can distinguish one group of buyers from another. Groups with significantly different responses or accessibility may best be defined with reference to a combination of psycho-social, purchasing, economic and other characteristics. However, an un-discriminating approach is very demanding of information from each buyer analysed.

Success in identifying segments is only part of the story, because for market planning purposes the stability of segments over time (how they grow, decline or merge) needs to be established. This requires determin-ing the explanatory factors for groupings of buyer characteristics. Unless there is reason to assume high segmental stability, the factors included in the segmentation analysis should themselves be forecastable. Such a restriction will impose a bias in favour of standard economic variables as opposed to psycho-social variables.

Carrying segmentation analysis through to its final stage requires establishing the degree of responsiveness of each segment to the product–marketing mix offered by the firm and its competitors. This requires use of the approaches discussed in Chapters 5 and 7.

CLASSIFICATION BY COMPETITIVE STRUCTURE

Although for short-term market planning purposes, the individual firm has little option but to accept the competitive structure within which it operates, over the long term it may be able – through product and market choice decisions – to involve itself in markets with substantially different degrees of competitiveness from its existing markets. The structure of competition is important because it affects the firm's ability to realise its business aims through marketing policy by determining the kinds of competitive policies it is likely to have to adopt to succeed. Let us therefore consider some general aspects of the relationship between market structure and business performance.

Using concentration (sometimes together with barriers to entry) as a measure of market structure, a number of studies of the relationship of market structure to performance have been carried out. On the whole, evidence suggests that higher levels of concentration are associated (but not very strongly) with higher profitability.[3] The relationship may not be straightforward. For example, when concentration reaches very high levels (say, for example, the top eight firms accounting for 70 per cent or more of output), then profitability may rise more significantly.[4] This may depend upon the relative size of firms that are included in the 'top' classification. The market share of firms from the fifth to the eigth may be important in reducing profitability.[5] This suggests that whatever the market share of the top four or so firms, the existence of several more firms of significant size may upset the structure of the competing group.

Even if higher concentration levels do open up the opportunity for making higher profits by exploiting the relative absence of competition, the efficiency of input use may be reduced and this may reduce the profitability of firms.[6] The lack of competitive pressure on prices may allow firms to be slack in their control over the use of resources. This suggests that firms in concentrated industries should pay special attention to cost control. It also implies that profit opportunities for very efficient firms may be very good in concentrated industries. However, if concentration arises from the possession of relatively scarce resources (such as management skills, R and D skills, prime retailing sites) then the price of these resources may rise to wipe out any extra profits.

Most concentration analyses are carried out with respect to national markets. The definition may be too broad (where markets are re-gionalised or localised) or too narrow (where the product group is widely traded internationally).[7] It is therefore important to take into account changes that may occur in the geographical characteristics of competition (for instance large increases in importing). This may be of major importance for the character of competition, for the behaviour of outsiders may (through different objectives, strategies and codes of managerial behaviour) be exceptionally unsettling to the market.[8]

The level of concentration may give some indication of the nature of competitive interaction and of the profitability to be expected in a given market. However, concentration levels may change considerably over relatively short periods of time. In the UK, for example, the one hundred largest (by output) firms in the manufacturing sector were responsible for 21 per cent of net manufacturing output in 1949, but 52 per cent by 1970.[9] This change in aggregate concentration was reflected in sub-stantial changes in concentration in individual industries.[10] The take-over of firms by other firms in the same industry, relatively rapid growth of larger firms and increasing barriers to entry are among the factors that account for increased concentration. Either basic economic factors (for instance economies of scale in production, distribution, purchasing or finance) or administrative factors (government policies to encourage mergers in particular industries on the grounds of real or imagined economies of scale) could explain increased concentration.

Entry barriers and performance in markets Entry barriers affect business performance by making entry more difficult and expensive (leading to reduced profits in firms trying to break into markets), probably increasing the profitability of firms already established behind the barriers, and increasing the likelihood of growth in concentration in the market. The nature of entry barriers in a particular market affects the kind of entry that may take place and the relative profitability of the enclosed market.[11] However, the relationship between barriers to entry and profitability needs to be judged with caution. Reported rates of return on capital may be distorted by accounting treatment of assets that contribute specifically to barriers to entry (such as R and D or goodwill created by advertising) as current outlays.[12] In addition, the use of entry-preventing pricing (limit pricing) as a barrier to entry may depress current profitability measures. Most studies show some kind of relationship between barriers to entry and profitability, although there is wide divergence in findings concerning the effects of barriers of different sizes.[13]

Although the relationship between business performance and competitive structure is obviously very complex, it is still worth trying to make use of it in long-term market planning decisions. Therefore, in assessing particular markets, marketing management should analyse how competitive structure has changed in the past, what barriers to entry exist and what their effect has been, how competitive structure is likely to evolve and how this is likely to affect profitability.

CRITERIA FOR MARKET CHOICE

The straightforward economic view is that market choice decisions should be taken in the same way as product line decisions or investment decisions – namely, on a discounted cash flow basis (if the information is available) modified if necessary by taking into account non-profit business aims. Allocation of output between different markets may be undertaken by using programming techniques, assuming information availability. However, given that information about long-term market prospects is not usually up to the standard required for the use of such techniques, normative approaches (such as those used for product choice) are frequently employed. There is a variety of general market characteristics which may be used as normative criteria for choosing amongst markets. Here, we shall analyse four ways of defining market choice criteria: market size, rate of growth of market, degree of difference of a market from the firm's existing market and number of markets.

SIZE OF MARKET

Market size is a conditional concept. The volume of business that may be achieved for a given product is conditional on the policies that are adopted to market it. The volume of business that may be reached in a given user need area is also conditional on the product designs offered by firms. The market for a product of a given design overlaps with the markets for its close substitutes (in other words buyers' demand clusters overlap). Slight changes in the economic environment, in marketing policy, in technologies or in preferences can therefore cause a given product's market to expand or contract significantly. Significant unsatisfied demand may exist because of short-term supply shortages or the absence of appropriate product offerings. Potential markets may be turned into actual markets by technical change, while actual markets may shrink because of the development of substitutes. Given these points, market revenue should be used as a measure of market size only with great care. It is also important to distinguish between the price and the quantity components of market revenue.

The attractiveness of a market depends on its size relative to the scale of operation needed to reap production, marketing or other economies of scale and relative to the size of firms involved or considering being involved in the market. The importance of efficient scale of operation depends upon the mode of involvement in a market (for example indirect selling, direct selling, assembly or manufacturing, with existing or with new products) and on factors such as the geographical dispersion of customers in a particular market, the variety of product needs and other such factors which determine the potential for exploiting scale economies. Whatever the costs involved in setting up market operations,[14] the ease of exploiting economies of scale also depends on ease of market penetration, size of barriers to entry and the defensive policies likely to be followed by firms already in the market. For example, entry into a market may only be feasible if the firm concentrates on specific service or product combinations which established firms do not offer. Such a policy may only be profitable for a small firm not dependent on exploiting economies of scale. However, the prospects for exploiting demand at the 'interstices of the market' may be better in larger markets.[15] In small markets, dominant firms may want to supply all buyer demands. However, in product areas characterised by domination by multinational firms, smaller national markets – in which no one major supplier dominates – may offer better prospects.

MARKET GROWTH RATES

The importance of market growth rate depends on its relationship to overall economic growth and to the growth rate of markets in which the firm is currently involved. Let us consider two kinds of situation: i) the market is located in another economy and is growing (together with the rest of that economy) faster than the firm's existing markets and ii) the market is growing faster than the economy/economies in which it is located and faster than the firm's existing markets.

Growth at the same rate as the economy In this situation the net result of the secular factors at work in the economy (income growth, economic development, technological change, evolution of preferences, etc.) does not especially favour the product group or (in the case of industrial products) products which use the product group as inputs. This may imply that the market is unlikely to attract entry from firms in other industries (unless these are in relative decline). If the firm considering entry into the market has some special advantage over established firms (for example lower price based on higher efficiency or lower input costs or better product design) then the firm may be able to achieve a stable addition to its sales, although short run profitability may be depressed temporarily because the firm has to engage in initial promotional activities. However, even if the firm possesses some advantage, it is important to analyse the reasons for the stability of the market relative to the economy in which it is located. The market may be passing through a maturity stage on its way to decline or just about to reach take-off. It may be ripe for a major technical advance, because firms already in the market have failed to engage in enough market and technological development.

Faster growth than the economy In this case, the net result of secular factors is to favour the demand for the product group or for products using the product group as an input. Here, the market situation may be more fluid. Firms already in the market will be working hard to capture as much of the growing market as possible, firms will be attracted from other industries, and new firms may be created to serve the market. These factors may lead the level of concentration to fall, implying a greater openness to entry.[16] The empirical evidence on this is conflicting,[17] but there is some substance to the view that concentration is least likely to decrease in industries characterised by high product differentiability.[18] Firms most likely to benefit from rapid market growth in a market characterised by high product differentiability are those with well established brands and large market shares. They find it easier to attract capital and the other resources needed for expansion, while market growth is channelled into their products by the strength of their franchise. Over the long run, however, any initial increase in concentration may be reversed as entry succeeds.[19] In markets characterised by low product differentiability, entry may be easier and concentration may be expected to fall.[20] In general markets that are growing relative to the economy may offer greater overall chances of success, but given the lack of stability of competitive structure and of buyer preferences likely to be associated with this growth, they may be riskier.

DIFFERENCE FROM FIRM'S EXISTING MARKETS

Differences between the firm's existing markets and the market under examination may relate to (i) the reasons for the existence, growth rate, etc., of the market; (ii) the techniques and facilities for marketing, distribution, etc., that are appropriate to the market; and (iii) the political and social environment of the market. Differences as a result of these factors may mean that the firm's resources cannot easily be adapted to serving the market, while acquiring the resources necessary to serve the market may be difficult (hence the resort to joint ventures, licensing, etc.).

The factors that explain the existence of demand differ from market to market and produce differences in buyer behaviour among markets. For example, a given product may be a luxury in one country, a necessity in another. Differences in buyer behaviour affect how well the firm is placed to supply what is required in each market, so that while the firm is used to supplying one kind of customer and has developed the resources and skills necessary to do so, these resources and skills may not be appropriate for other markets.

However, differences in the underlying causes of demand can be an advantage if a firm needs to spread risk, because the more diverse the origins of demand, the less likely that all markets will be adversely affected by particular factors.

The decision to sell in a particular market may not be directly related to sales or profitability but rather a question of some contribution by the market to the firm's market and product learning. A market may contain a group of sophisticated buyers who are the source of many new product ideas, improvements, etc. Learning from these buyers may enable the firm to do well in its other markets.[21]

In its existing markets, a firm uses a particular combination of marketing and distribution methods. Each method requires different skills and capabilities on the part of management, different levels of responsiveness in production and physical distribution, and so forth. In new markets, different distribution and marketing patterns may be appropriate, and these will make different demands upon management. The flexibility of the firm in the face of such demands needs to be taken into account in market diversification decisions.

Political and social factors exercise their influence partly through the above groups of factors. In some markets, it may be particularly difficult (or easy) for a particular firm to operate because of its ability to deal with the political and social impediments to marketing. This may amount to no more than knowing when and where to give inducements or a common ethnic or cultural bond with customers.

NUMBER OF MARKETS

If a firm assesses each market independently of other markets, it has to be prepared to diffuse its marketing effort over a large number of markets. As an alternative to this, it may adopt a policy of concentrating on key markets. General arguments relating to concentration in key markets refer to economies or diseconomies of scale in marketing or risk spreading.[22] Economies of scale in marketing may result from the existence of a marketing threshold (determined by marketing set-up costs) or of declining unit marketing costs for a given marketing system, but changes to more efficient marketing systems as degree of involvement in a market increases may be more important (e.g. moving from order-broking agent through agents who take title to wholly owned sales subsidiaries). Diseconomies of scale may arise from high costs of maintaining or increasing market share in the face of competitors' policies or demand limitations. If the marketing budget is limited, then it may pay to diffuse marketing effort unless the threshold effect is too strong.

The need for a firm to spread risk depends not just on its ability to absord the consequences of coincident bad performance but also on its effect on long-term strategy. Risk spreading should therefore be undertaken not just on the basis of likely coincidence of detrimental factors in the short term but also on the basis of the contribution of particular markets to long-term aims.

MARKET CHOICE – DECIDING TO DECIDE

Marketing management needs to beware of the tendency for markets to 'evolve' rather than to be chosen according to their likely contribution to the firm's aims and strategies. Sometimes, through customers approaching the firm, 'natural' extensions of the firm's activities (whether on a geographical or customer needs basis) and so forth, a firm may find itself with a set of markets which are not appropriate to its aims and strategies. It is therefore important for management to carry out a 'market inventory check' from time to time to assess the contribution of each market. This requires running a check not only on current profitability, sales and costs, but also on likely future developments in technology, competitive structure, buyer needs and behaviour, government policy, exchange rates, contribution to technical and market learning, and so on.

10 Pricing

Pricing policies affect the performance of individual products and businesses and are also symptomatic of and may determine market structure. Economic analysis of pricing policy starts by analysing the effect of price on the quantity demanded (the price elasticity of demand). Because the quantity demanded is related to the quantity produced, and because unit costs may be affected by the quantity produced, price changes may lead to cost changes. Since most firms face competition of some kind, price changes on the part of one firm may provoke response from other firms, either in the form of of price changes or changes in other elements of the marketing mix. The net effect of a price change (taking into account cost changes and competitive interaction) is evaluated in terms of the firm's business aims.

Taking into account the analysis of the foregoing chapters, we can say that the advisability of particular pricing policies depends upon the following factors:

CUSTOMER FACTORS

1. Responsiveness of buyers and potential buyers (singly or in groups) to price changes (price elasticity of demand), in short and long run.

2. Responsiveness of buyers and potential buyers (singly or in groups) to changes in other elements of the marketing mix (substitutability of other elements of the marketing mix for pricing).

FACTORS INTERNAL TO THE FIRM

3. Aims, goals and strategies of the firm, as they affect products for which pricing policy is under consideration.

4. Cost considerations, including how costs are affected by changes in the scale and mix of output caused by pricing policy and policies that are used as complements or substitutes for pricing policy.

COMPETITIVE FACTORS

5. Short and long-run responses of competitors to changes in the firm's marketing mix.

6. Evolution of the structure of the industry in which the firm operates, and how this affects and is affected by the firm's pricing policy.

Let us consider these factors in turn.

CUSTOMER FACTORS

In Chapter 5, it was pointed out that price is one of a number of characteristics possessed by a product. The individual or industrial buyer decides whether to purchase a product on the basis of an evaluation of how a product's set of characteristics compares with those of other products, given the set of characterisitcs that the buyer demands from the product. The effect of price therefore depends upon the prices charged for competing products and (where competing products are not identical) on the other characteristics of competing products relative to the product in question. Given these points, it is important for marketing management to establish the trade-off rate between price and product–marketing characteristics. Even if products are identically specified in the technical sense, there is room for differentiation on service, distribution, and so on. Without establishing trade-off rates, it is impossible to predict how products with particular prices will fare in the face of changes in other elements of the marketing mix and in competitors' policies.

For marketing policy purposes, it is rarely enough to take all potential customers, gather data on their preferences and/or on their buying behaviour and subject it to statistical analysis to establish the rate of trade-off between price and other characteristics. There is usually no such thing as *one* market and *one* price. Nor is it likely that the information possessed by buyers and potential buyers about price is anything like perfect. So the first step in the empirical analysis of responsiveness to price should be prior segmentation by price awareness. Empirical research has shown a surprising lack of price awareness, among both consumers and industrial goods buyers.[1] This may be because buyers do not recall the prices of alternative products, because they do not trouble to obtain the information (this possibly extending beyond price to information on all product characterisitcs), because the price package presented to the buyer is too complicated for him to analyse (especially common with credit purchases), because the buyer's knowledge on prices has become outdated, or because the product itself is too complicated for a single price to be tied to it (particularly common in some service sectors). Lack of price awareness may turn what might have been a highly competitive market (given the number of firms, the products produced and so on) into a market in which it is possible to engage in substantial price discrimination among customers on the basis of price awareness. Competitive advantage is likely to go to the firm most able to exploit this situation (that is to say the firm which does the appropriate market research and has a flexible enough pricing system for it to discriminate in this way). If substantial segments of the market are found to be unaware of prices, advantage may also go to the firm that is able to sell more cheaply and able to ensure that appropriate price information is absorbed by buyers. For this strategy to be employed, it is important to analyse exactly why buyers do lack price awareness.

Assuming the market to have been segmented by price awareness, the next step may be to segment the market by product characteristics awareness. As price is only one of the criteria used by buyers for assessing products, it follows that buyer awareness of other product characteristics will also affect the impact of price. In some cases, buyers may simply ignore competitive products (without obtaining information on their prices or other characteristics), either through straightforward inertia or because of strong brand loyalty (interpreted as a conviction that no other product could match the product currently being bought). Here, the marketing problem is not a price problem. In other cases, price may be used as an indicator of quality, in the absence of any other easy indicator.[2] Here, it is important to establish empirically under exactly what conditions price is used in this way, in particular whether the explanation is to be found in lack of information provision by manufacturers, strong promotional association of price and quality, or some other factor.

In some product areas, price cannot be represented by a single figure. This may be due to discounting policies of manufacturers or distributors, inclusion in the purchase price of additional items (such as service or accessories), or the method used to provide financing for the purchase. In any research into the effects of price, it is important to ensure that the appropriate measures are used. This may imply (in the case of a product sold on credit, for example) separation of price into down-payment and instalment.

Before attempting to quantify the sensitivity of demand to price, it is important to take into account the above points. Once the market has been segmented as described above, standard multivariate statistical techniques can be used to establish the importance of price. Estimates of the price elasticity of demand for particular firm's products should be treated with care. Although elasticities for broad product classes tend to show some stability over time, this is partly because they are unaffected by competitive factors. The impact of price on market share may be subject to substantial changes if competitive policies are specifically aimed at destabilising market structure (e.g. through new product policy).

FACTORS INTERNAL TO THE FIRM

In Chapter 2 we discussed how the aims, goals and strategies of the firm might be related to policy. Empirical research on objectives as applied to pricing has suggested that even for this most fundamental policy area, there is often confusion about what objectives the firm should follow when it sets its prices.[3] Pricing is a policy area where marketing management is most likely to come into conflict with other functions, particularly finance. The feeling that prices should be discounted to ensure the achievement of sales goals has to be set against the damage to contribution this may cause (and consequent risk of not achieving profit goals). For this reason it is particularly important to ensure that pricing policy makers are well informed about the company's objectives and about the procedures to be followed in cases of conflict.

In Chapter 6 we analysed a situation in which the procedure for calculating costs had an important impact on the acceptability of a particular price. In general costing policies exercise an important impact on pricing because of the widespread use of mark-up pricing policies. If a firm uses a cost-plus pricing system, then this is likely to reduce its sensitivity to demand conditions. Recent research confirms that in many industries, prices are relatively insensitive to changes in demand.[4] Economists have devoted considerable time to discussion of whether firms that avowedly follow cost-plus pricing policies in practice adjust mark-ups to allow for demand factors. For example, a price which is fixed on the basis of a particular mark-up normally has to remain constant for a period in which output variations take place. Given that unit costs are affected by output variations, higher demand will produce higher margins in industries characterised by economies of scale. From the marketing point of view, the cost-plus argument is only important because it demonstrates that a manager's perception of what he is doing (in particular how he is pricing) may be strongly at variance with the actual situation. There are undoubtedly strong administrative reasons for adopting cost-plus policies. In industries with high capital equipment requirements and where equipment is used to produce many different kinds of products, the only way of ensuring that a rate of return on capital aim is met may be to calculate the capital–output ratio and use the desired profits rate to reach a desired profit–output ratio. This procedure has the disadvantage that if the capital–output ratio for a particular product is significantly different from the average for the firm, pricing by the use of an overall mark-up may exclude a profitable product (because its price as calculated is too high) or allow an unprofitable product through.

More sophisticated methods of capital budgeting and cost reporting may reduce the extent to which cost-plus pricing has to be relied on as a second best. Because some firms operate with aims that are related to rate of return on capital, it is important for pricing to be considered in conjunction with investment analysis. As there are likely to be problems with the allocation of overheads, it may be possible to integrate pricing and investment analysis fully only with new products. With new products, it may be possible to consider the new product project as an investment project, and analyse the effects of different prices (and different marketing mix combinations) on the rate of return on capital from the project, although such a procedure is very demanding of information.

COMPETITIVE FACTORS

The standard economic models of competitive structure help to explain how pricing policies are affected by the nature of demand, costs and the nature of competition. Without repeating too much basic material, it will help to review their basic conclusions here. In the perfectly competitive situation, prices are entirely determined by costs, since in the long run competition forces prices down to where it just pays firms to stay in business, taking into account the cost of capital and the cost of entrepreneurial skill. Once an element of product differentiation appears, the situation becomes one of imperfect or monopolistic competition. Depending on the structure of demand (in particular, the diversity of requirements) and on the economics of production, each producer produces a slightly different variant, which it does not pay any other producer to imitate exactly. However, price is still entirely determined by costs, for any excess profits (higher price—marginal cost ratio) are whittled away by competitors producing similar but not identical products. If the number of competitors is restricted (for example through any barrier to entry), then the tie between costs and prices becomes less automatic, and prices are in addition affected by firms' business aims, policies followed with regard to other elements of the marketing mix, and so on. In the case of monopoly, the absence of competition creates a situation in which the relationship between price and costs is entirely determined by costs and business aims. If there is the possibility of entry by other firms, then pricing policy may be moderated to take this into account.

Let us now consider the marketing implications of each of these situations, starting with monopoly. If the firm is a sole supplier and there is no risk of entry by other firms or of intervention by public authorities, then the appropriate policy to follow will normally be one of price discrimination. The overall output level (and thus the average price charged) will be determined by the general relation between demand and cost conditions (for example substantial economies of scale or highly elastic demand are likely to weigh in favour of a lower price). For a given output level, higher revenue can be obtained by separating markets and charging higher prices in markets where the price elasticity of demand is lower (a policy that would be inhibited in other market situations by the existence of competition). This requires segmenting the market, in particular with respect to responsiveness to price and with respect to separability of the market (for example accessibility through a different distribution system). Systematic market analysis should also take into account the possibility of discriminating among customers by offering different combinations of product characteristics.

In monopolistic situations (whether in local, regional or national markets) there usually is a price level above which entry by other firms would take place. If this is so, then pricing policy should take into account the profit implications of prices for potential competitors (given entry costs). It may be appropriate to set an entry-deterring or limit price,[5] the height of which depends not only on straightforward cost factors but also on the strength of the existing firm's customer franchise. In such situations it is appropriate for the monopolistic firm to consider its market as potentially oligopolistic.

In oligopolistic markets, where the actions of each firm may have a significant effect on other firms, pricing policy depends on the extent of product differentiation. For undifferentiated (commodity) products, where the only factors that help a firm to keep its place in the market are the existence of an established marketing network and (in some cases) economies of scale, price competition may be highly destabilising, for the availability of the product at a lower price elsewhere may cause a firm to lose most of its customers. In such a situation, it may be best to move to some kind of co-operative pricing arrangement. This may be an informal arrangement, an example of which is price leadership,[6] in which one or more firms are regarded as price leaders and the rest follow. This arrangement may evolve purely for administrative reasons. In a period of inflation, when the costs of all firms in a particular market may be rising more or less at equal rates, then the timing of price rises may pose a problem as far as the stability of market structure is concerned. Differentials may be opened up which are inconvenient to all parties (even for those whose prices remain temporarily low, since demand for the products of these firms may be greater than can be supplied from full capacity production, and orders may have to be taken at current prices, to be met with higher cost production later on). In such cases, it may be easier for all concerned to follow the dominant firm.[7] Price leadership may also be useful in situations of fluctuating demand. If there is a risk of government intervention, it may be a useful way of providing a shelter for less efficient firms.

If market conditions make informal price co-operation unreliable, more formal price fixing (and associated output allocation) may be appropriate. However, the long-term advantages of formal price fixing are not always clear. The costs to the individual firm for the product in question may be higher or lower than the average of the competing group. If the firm's costs are higher than average, then a co-operative arrangement may be the only way in which it can survive until it takes steps to raise its efficiency. This depends upon whether the joint price has been fixed so as to yield very high profits for the most efficient firms. If the firm's costs are lower than average, then a decision has to be made on how the firm should exploit its greater efficiency. Depending on the availability of investment capital, the strength of its marketing and its business aims, the firm may want to go for high profits on low turnover by co-operating, or it may want to try to capture a larger market share by competing on price in the expectation that at a later stage some competitors will be forced out of the market. If the latter policy is adopted, then the firm must be sure that it can preserve its relative efficiency under changed competitive conditions.

The advisability of formal co-operation on price also depends partly on the firm's strength in other marketing variables. If a firm ties its hands on price, it may need to rely on other competitive weapons to maintain its market position. The marketing strengths required will depend upon the characteristics of the market in question. Strength in product design, for example, may be no substitute for selling strength.

Co-operation on price is likely to be appropriate in situations of high buyer concentration. This may occur with respect to distributors. Given that buyers in such situations may be very well informed about costs and likely to be able to exploit any differences between competing suppliers, co-operation may be difficult to enforce.

Whether pricing agreements are reached or not, pricing in oligopolistic markets remains a point of high competitive sensitivity. For this reason, competition may focus on quality (the characteristics that are built into products). Because quality is in a sense the inverse of price, care may have to be taken not to market price – quality combinations that offer too obvious a reduction in price per unit quality. Suppose, for example, that the two principal qualities embodied in a product are X and Y, and that one firm wants to embody a substantially greater amount of X in its product than other products in the same price range. To do this may provoke substantial price retaliation, so it may be appropriate to offer in addition substantially more Y and move the product into a higher price range. The feasibility of such a policy depends on the exact nature of demand for product characteristics, of course.

In oligopolistic markets, the implications of pricing for competitive structure may be a dominant consideration in price fixing. The relationship between price and cost will determine incentives to enter or leave the industry. Given the link between barriers to entry, concentration and profitability, price must be seen as one of a range of ways of defending or exploiting competitive positions. Limit pricing may be used with particular effectiveness if it is possible to discriminate among customers such that competition can be fended off in certain segments of the market without reducing the profitability of sales in other markets. In some markets, responsiveness to promotion or selling effort may indicate a policy of charging high prices and defending the market by promotion or sales effort. Given the substitutability of pricing for other marketing policies, it is particularly important not to allow pricing flexibility to be affected by particular rules relating price to cost. Such rules not only affect current success, but may also allow competitive structure to change against the firm's interest.

In situations of imperfect or monopolistic competition, the individual firm has little control over price because competitors are free to produce similar products: marketing similar products is assumed to raise no particular problems of entry. In such situations, there is a premium on finding price –characteristics combinations which are profitable but not worth the while of other firms to imitate because of the limited size of the market for the combination. This implies that successful marketing is highly dependent on accurate market research (as well as on innovating in creating new combinations). As far as price is concerned, this means establishing in detail how customers in different segments of the market trade off price against other characteristics. In such a situation there is also a premium on research into the combinations offered or likely to be offered by close competitors.

In situations of perfect competition, because of the assumptions of freedom of entry, product identicality and availability of all resources on the same terms to all producers, prices are dictated by the market. However, pricing is only completely automatic in situations where the market has reached equilibrium (in other words where suppliers have fully adjusted to demand and technological conditions). In markets where demand is continually changing in character and in product areas where technologies of production or design are subject to frequent change, adjustment to new structures of demand or technologies may never be complete. In such situations, pricing policy is no longer simply a question of charging the going market rate. Positions of temporary oligopoly or monopoly are being created all the time, and although entry by other firms is guaranteed, there will be opportunities to exploit these temporary situations. From the pricing point of view, this implies obtaining appropriate information about price – characteristics trade-offs for use in situations where the nature of demand changes or where technological change enables product design changes to be made. Such information provides the basis for price discrimination until imitation takes place. In situations where technological change leads to reduced costs, the appropriate pricing policy may be maintenance of price until other firms apply the changes in technology.

PRICING THROUGH THE DISTRIBUTION SYSTEM

Whatever the competitive structure of the industry, many firms are faced with the problem of how to price through the distribution system. In some market areas, there are well-established discount structures. These structures are only rarely completely rigid. In most cases, they are subject to change under the pressures of competition and structural change in the industries concerned. Changing demand patterns and product ranges also create pressure for change. Discounts tend to reflect the functions that distributors perform (see Chapter 12), but the functions that they need to perform change under the above-mentioned influences. For example, a new product which achieves major market success and more or less sells itself, reducing the distributors' tasks of providing information and advice, reducing the selling effort needed on the part of distributors and possibly increasing their rate of stock turnover, may allow for the negotiation of a lower discount to distributors. Distributors may resist pressure to cut discounts, arguing that lower turnover or more problematic items be given substantially higher discounts. Because of this it may be appropriate for firms in weaker bargaining positions to stay within the established discount structure. Firms in stronger positions should, in taking discount decisions, take account of distributors' cost structures and of the profitability implications for distributors of different discount structures, just as in normal pricing decisions buyers' demand is taken into account.

PRICING OVER TIME

If the industry is one in which there are major fluctuations in demand or supply, a time-based discount structure may be used. This raises no special problems of economic principle. If it is possible to discriminate between the time periods concerned, the profit maximising firm will adjust its price and output in each period such that marginal cost and marginal revenue are equal in each period. In practice application of this or similar principles is likely to require modification to take into account shifting of demand between time periods and – in the case where intermediaries are used to sell the product – shifting of supply between time periods. In addition there may be problems with customer goodwill if price changes between time periods are too great. The structure of competition will affect the individual firm's ability to impose price structures aimed at moulding demand to supply. The existence of competitors with spare capacity can be particularly destabilising in industries where demand fluctuates, for each firm may treat off-peak periods as purely marginal, with prices being cut to close to marginal cost levels.

QUANTITY DISCOUNTS

In some cases, quantity discounts have their origin in historical differences in costs, in customer requirements and in distribution systems. In general quantity discounts are given either as a way of passing on economies of scale to customers or as a way of discriminating among customers. The existence of economies of scale does not by itself imply that quantity discounts are advisable. This depends upon the competitive situation – namely whether such discounts will give the firm a competitive edge or enable it to preserve its competitive position and what the risks are that such discounts will be interpreted as general price cuts which provoke retaliation. Price cuts in the form of quantity discounts may be an appropriate way of using limit pricing as a barrier to entry.

If the market is characterised by major differences in the volume of purchases among customers, then the pressure that larger buyers exercise on suppliers may be formalised through quantity discounts. In such situations it is important for suppliers to consider what real alternatives are available to customers. No matter how important the customer, if he has no real possibility of buying elsewhere it may be possible to moderate quantity discounts.

PRICING IN BARGAINING SITUATIONS

In some situations, the price of a product is not fixed beforehand but is subject to bargaining between buyer and seller. This question is covered in detail in Chapter 12. Here, we note that in such situations, management needs to analyse two aspects: namely the upper and lower limits to price and the determinants of bargaining strength, which affects where the price is fixed within these limits. Upper limits are fixed by buyer benefit, while lower limits are fixed by cost conditions. The size of the deal negotiated will affect both limits. Strengths and weaknesses in bargaining are determined by the importance of the deal being negotiated, the price and conditions of alternative deals available to buyer or seller, the costs to either side if the deal were completely abandoned and the implications of success or failure in concluding the deal for supplier–buyer relationships. These factors depend in turn on competitive structures, cost structures and organisational factors.

PRICING IN BID SITUATIONS

Bid situations resemble bargaining situations in that the price is being fixed for a particular supplier–customer deal. However, the existence of an invitation to tender suggests that there is a high probability that the deal has to be concluded. Sellers therefore have the additional information that the buyer is unlikely to settle for the alternative of not making a deal. However, the seller also knows that the publication of the invitation to tender will bring other firms into the market. The seller is at a disadvantage in that he has no exact information about the prices quoted by competitors, but he does know exactly what has to be supplied and who is likely to be able to supply it. This knowledge creates the opportunity for collusion. Quotes on particular bids may be arranged as part of a series of quotes designed to ensure that business is shared out in a particular way. If no collusive arrangement is possible, then the individual firm may try to predict the bids of its competitors. Various methods have been suggested for this,[8] mostly relating bids to past bids in similar situation, taking into account information about whether competitors are achieving their market share or other targets, their cost situation, and so on.

TRANSFER PRICING

A problem faced by firms selling to firms which belong to the same parent company, to subsidiaries or to parent companies themselves is that of fixing a price for the transfer such that the firm's business achievement is not adversely affected. The problem is caused by conflict between the demands of accounting, legal or taxation systems and the demands of management systems. Different tax rates, either on profits or on the products, different tax regulations, subsidy arrangements and so on, may make it more profitable for profit or sales to be located in a particular company, country, region, etc. This means that transfer prices may be manipulated to the company's advantage. Assuming no other problems (say, for instance, authorities enquiries into reasons for continuing losses in a particular subsidiary), all pricing calculations should be made net of all taxes, (including profits tax) subsidies, etc. This may raise administrative problems for the company, because it involves treating each price as part of a pricing system.

The managerial problem is slightly more complicated. If the most profitable pricing policy (for tax reasons) is one which involves continual losses in a particular subsidiary, there may be problems of motivation amongst the management of the subsidiary. Such problems may be averted by adding back the appropriate sums in managerial calculations. More detailed problems are likely to arise where particular products are concerned. Some firms underprice products which are transferred between divisions in order to ensure that the price of their final product is competitive. This may raise problems in evaluating efficiency and may produce complaints from competitors who are less integrated. Other firms leave the price to be determined to bargaining among the companies concerned. If the product being transferred is not available on the open market, then the situation becomes one of bilateral monopoly, and the outcome will be determined by the bargaining considerations discussed in Chapter 12. If the product is one which is also available on the open market, firms may price according to the market price. This is appropriate if the market is competitive, but if the market for the product is not competitive, while the market for the firm's end product is, some competitive advantage may be lost (there will be some sales which the firm could make at a lower price if it adopted a transfer price for the intermediate product which was more closely related to costs). In principle, whatever the firm's business aims and whatever the competitive situation in the markets for intermediate and final products, it is appropriate to transfer products at prices in which the marginal costs, overhead costs and profits are separately identifiable. This enables decisions about the final price to be made on the basis of full knowledge about the impact of final sales on profits, costs, etc.[9]

NEW PRODUCT PRICING

For a new product the price performs several different functions. The price that is fixed for a new product affects customers' first perceptions of the product relative to existing products and may signal quality. It indicates how much the buyer has to spend in order to experience the product. Consequently, in introducing a new product, it is important for the firm to be well-informed on how prices affect sampling behaviour of innovative buyers, who may provide the key to the diffusion process. Depending on the firm's sales objectives, on the relation between the production capacity for the product and estimated market size, on the likely speed of diffusion and on the likeness of competitive imitation, the firm may decide on skimming, penetration or some intermediate pricing policy.[10] Mixing the strategies among different markets or different products may be chosen by the risk-avoiding firm. It is important to consider new product pricing within the context of the firm's overall product strategy. A firm which has specialised in mass produced products, which it has always launched on a penetration price, will not always find it easy to switch to a skimming policy on a new product, for in skimming, the emphasis must be on finding premium customers and giving them the appropriate service level.

ECONOMIC APPROACHES TO PRICING

The main problems in pricing are not problems of principle but empirical problems. It is clear that in pricing decisions, it is important to take into account the relationship between price, quantity demanded, output, costs and profitability, the relationship between the firm's price and competitors' marketing policies, the relationship between price and other elements of the firm's marketing mix (and, where appropriate, prices of other products marketed by the firm), the relationship between price and industry structure, and the rate of trade-off between price and other product characteristics. Obtaining the information required is principally a question of empirical research. On the demand side, firms should not be satisfied with overall price responsiveness statistics but should undertake segmentation analyses to establish differences in price sensitivity in different parts of the market. Where costs are concerned, it is important that figures should be available on a marginal and on an opportunity cost basis. The most serious empirical problems occur in situations of competition among a few firms, where competitive responses to price changes may be highly unpredictable. However, even here, statistical analysis of past responses and the conditions under which they occurred may give an adequate guide to policy.

11 Promotion

Economic analyses of promotion have concentrated mainly on advertising and – to the extent that they are included in pricing analysis – promotional discounts. All above-the-line promotional methods share the same general characteristic that they involve the purchase or use of services (and sometimes goods) in an attempt to increase or maintain sales (i.e. shifting the demand curve outwards or maintaining its position). Corporate advertising may be an exception to this, especially where it is associated with the raising of capital. Most of the analysis in this chapter will apply to advertising, but the methodologies can on the whole be applied to all above-the-line methods. Economic analysis has been applied to the more theoretical issue of the conditions in which it is worthwhile engaging in promotion and to the empirical issue of the productivity or yield of advertising.

ADVERTISING INTENSITY – GENERAL ISSUES

Many of the issues concerning the worthwhileness of advertising involve discussion of advertising intensity, which is defined as the relationship between advertising expenditure and turnover. If we assume that firms spend on advertising according to productivity, then the substantial differences that exist between advertising expenditure : sales ratios in different industries suggests that managerial assessments of advertising intensity should relate to firms in the same industry, although this poses a problem for multi-industry firms. Given the relative constancy of advertising ratios for a given industry in different countries, there may be forces at work which produce particular levels of advertising intensity in particular kinds of product market, suggesting that advertising is of limited substitutability for other elements of the marketing mix. Moves away from the industry advertising intensity may therefore be inhibited by this lack of substitutability.

The factors that affect the effectiveness of advertising (and hence its substitutability for other marketing policies) include the nature of the product, buyer characteristics and behaviour and the nature of competition. If the firm's product has characteristics which differentiate it from competing products, then advertising can be used to emphasise differences. Extent of differentiation in turn depends upon differentiability (affected by technical, legal and demand factors) and on the extent of exploitation of differentiability (affected by production factors – for example the economies to be gained by commitment to long production runs, and by competitive factors – how far competitive pressures force firms to exploit differentiability). Differentiation opens up opportunities for promotion to exercise its two major functions (persuading and informing) to the advantage of the product and the firm. Promotion may itself be the major source of differentiation.

The newness of a product affects the appropriateness of particular promotional levels, through the amount of information and experience possessed by the buyer. With completely new products, the potential buyer may be highly dependent on the firm for information and be especially susceptible to persuasion because of limited product experience. Persuasion is also very important for new products entering markets characterised by high brand loyalty and entrenched competition.

The nature of the production process for the product determines the importance of market stability. Processes involving heavy initial investment may require higher promotion to stabilise demand. This will be affected by the extent of product differentiability.

The effect of buyer characteristics and behaviour can be analysed through the nature of the potential buyer's demand for product characteristics. These characteristics include physical characteristics of the product (that is to say the 'objective' specifications of the product – in the case of a physical product, weight, dimensions, colour, capacity, etc.), characteristics related to the purchasing situation (for example kind of outlet, information supplied with the product, financial conditions of purchase) and less objectively specifiable characteristics (what we may call 'associative' characteristics, related to the image of the product and the supplier). The decision to purchase is a result of buyers receiving information about these different kinds of characteristic and evaluating the match between characteristics and demand. This process can be affected by promotion in various ways.

As far as providing information is concerned, it is important for the firm to establish in what situations provision of more information can help the firm to achieve its aims.[1] Markets therefore need to be analysed not simply in terms of the demand for physical and other characteristics in products, but also in terms of the demand by buyers for information and the supply of information that is reaching buyers about product characteristics, availability, etc. This analysis should be an integral part of the market segmentation process. The diffusion of information depends not just on the firm's efforts but also on social information diffusion processes and on the availability of media to transmit the required information. Informative advertising at high levels may be called for where a product is truly innovative, where the firm is seeking to create entirely new markets or where it seeks to penetrate existing markets by isolating segments where information diffusion has previously been inadequate.

The persuasive function of advertising can be separated into two different processes, the first relying upon changing the buyer's demand for product characteristics and the second upon persuading the potential buyer that the product's characteristics meet his requirements. As far as the first of these is concerned, marketing management needs to consider how promotion can be used to operate on the determinants of preferences. The second type of process may be required to overcome problems of uncertainty in the buying situation (which may be produced by lack of information or by lack of experience). In general the persuasive function of advertising is likely to have the most scope where preference patterns and hence purchasing decisions are most strongly affected by factors such as status, health and other personal considerations.[2]

The sensitivity of demand to price affects the use of promotion as a competitive weapon. In markets where buyers are highly responsive to price cuts, heavy promotional expenditure (however effective it might be if prices were fixed) may be made redundant by competitive price cutting. However, it is sometimes possible to combat price cutting by promotion specifically aimed at increasing the difference between products as perceived by buyers, thereby reducing the price elasticity of demand for the product. Even if the price elasticity of demand is already low, high promotional levels may be used to reinforce buyers' unwillingness to consider alternative products when they are cheaper.

Because firms use independent distributors in many consumer markets, promotional expenditure may be required to persuade distributors to stock and push the product. Advertising is partially a substitute for demonstrated success here, so it may be worthwhile attempting to demonstrate success in part of the market and using this to persuade rather than spending large amounts on distributors promotion from the outset.[3]

The nature of competition obviously has a substantial effect on advertising intensity.[4] In the monopolist's case, advertising is undertaken to increase or reinforce a tendency to buy the firm's product as opposed to the general run of products. With no question of retaliation or entry (by assumption), the promotional decision is a result of choosing between various profit-creating options, including other methods of shifting the demand curve outwards or making it more inelastic, as well as cost reduction policies. If there is a possibility of entry, then if the supplier or his product can be differentiated from competition, promotion is likely to be aimed at increasing the differentiation, although the cost reduction option may still be relatively attractive if it allows limit pricing to be used more effectively. The tendency to use promotion is likely to be reinforced by avoidance of price competition.[5] In situations approximating perfect competition, promotional intensity is unlikely to be high, although advertising as a carrier of information may have an important role to play. On these arguments, we should expect the relationship between advertising and industrial concentration (as a measure of competitive structure) to be non-linear, with low levels of advertising in highly concentrated and unconcentrated industries, but this hypothesis is only partly confirmed by empirical studies.[6] The lack of agreement in statistical studies is probably due to difficulty in finding variables to represent (in inter-industry studies) the other factors that explain advertising levels – product differentiability, production methods, buyer characteristics and barriers to entry.

EMPIRICAL ANALYSIS OF ADVERTISING AND PROMOTION

The effects of the nature of the product, the nature of the product and the nature of competition on the promotional decision are points that most marketing managers will take for granted. The real question facing them is the quantitative one – how much does advertising affect commercial success and how much should be budgeted for each product. Analysis at the level of the industry, firm and individual ·product can help to answer these questions.

ADVERTISING-PROFIT RELATIONSHIP AT THE INDUSTRY LEVEL

A basic question facing marketing management is how productive industry promotional practices really are. A number of studies have been carried out on the relationship between advertising and profitability.[7] Nearly all the studies find that the relationship between advertising and profitability is positive and statistically significant at the industry and – where tested – at the firm level. Although some of these studies encountered specification problems, such that the apparent effect of advertising on profitability may partly be due to excluded variables or reverse causation, latest studies have supported the original findings when the specification problems have been removed.[8] The majority of the empirical studies also suggest that much of the effect of advertising is not through a straightforward alteration of preferences towards particular products, leading to higher sales at given prices and higher profits due to economies of scale, or to higher prices leading directly to higher profits. If this were so, a substantial cancelling-out of effects would be expected in markets where advertising levels were matched by competing firms. Advertising seems to have its main impact through the erection or fortification of barriers to entry by new competition. This implies that advertising, as well as being affected by competitive structure, is also a major determinant of competitive structure.[9] Promotional decisions should therefore take into account _explicitly_ the extent to which competition can be regulated by the use of promotion.

The relationship between promotion and barriers to entry is not direct, such that the more spent on promotion, the higher the entry barrier created. Barriers are created not just by one firm's promotion but by the promotion of all firms in the competing group. The existence of a weak competitor, whose competitive policies do not provide good defence against entry, may open up entry possibilities. Promotional policies may in such situations be more effective if designed to close such openings by capturing the market of the weak firm.

The relationship between promotion and barriers to entry may also be characterised by threshold and saturation effects. The tendency to buy may be affected significantly if potential buyers are exposed to a certain amount of promotional activity, while over a certain level of exposure, the tendency to buy may not be further reinforced. Depending upon the distribution among the potential buyers of responsiveness to promotion, the cost of passing the threshold with enough potential buyers may constitute a major barrier to entry. Given cancelling out, the level of the threshold may be a relative one, depending upon total promotional volume in the market. If the saturation level is not too much higher than the threshold, firms already in the market may find promotional levels near the threshold all that is necessary to maintain competitive positions.

The creation of barriers to entry by promotion is a lagged process, which works through the creation and reinforcement of purchasing habits, through the alteration of buyer perceptions of products and suppliers and through the reinforcement of supplier credibility with distributors. Some promotional expenditure can be treated as strategic investment rather than as a way to increase immediate profitability. Although advertising–profitability coefficients may be taken as some indicator of the gains to be expected from advertising, it is perhaps safer to consider the benefits as long-term and budget accordingly. Note too that although inter-industry and inter-firm studies of advertising–profitability relationships produce coefficients which are in principle marginal (showing the effects of increased advertising on profitability, *ceteris paribus*), such coefficients should be interpreted with care in the light of the existence of economies or diseconomies of scale in promotion – both as far as purchasing and effectiveness are concerned – and threshold and saturation effects.

ANALYSIS AT THE PRODUCT LEVEL

There are many ways in which promotional messages may be transmitted. The impact of a given promotional budget depends upon the media used, the format, the details of the message, and so on. The market and advertising research literature contains many examples of analyses of different media according to various criteria of effectiveness (for example, number of potential buyers exposed to promotion, physiological phenomena associated with exposure to the promotion, or sales – where these can be directly attributed).[10] Studies have also been carried out on the effects of different ways of implementing media decisions (diffuse or intense promotion and timing of promotion according to phases of the product life cycle, for example).[11] The effects of advertising on different kinds of potential buyer or in different purchasing situations have also received considerable attention.[12] The economic contribution to the analysis of the effectiveness of different promotional mixes is limited.[13] Economic analyses tend to take promotional mix as given, although the principle of marginality has obvious relevance,[14] and to consider the relationship between advertising and sales on an aggregated basis.

The effect of advertising over time The effects of a given advertising action normally last for some time. This is for several reasons, including the durability of some forms of advertising (namely an advertisement in a magazine will continue to be read as long as the magazine lasts), the diffusion through the population of purchasing behaviour originally triggered by advertising, the deferment of the effect of the increased tendency to buy the product, caused by advertising (for example because the buyer was originally not in the right age or income group, because the product was originally not available through the appropriate distributor, because buyers' needs independently change in the direction of the general class of product, because the price of the product moves into a range which makes purchase feasible, etc.), the dependence of the effect on a cumulative impact process and the deferment of acceptance by some distributors until the product – aided by advertising – has reached a particular turnover level. If a Koyck transformation is used to handle the lagged effect of advertising, then it may be reasonable to assume that the relationship between the past and the present effects of advertising differs from that between past and present effects of other variables that determine sales.[15] One way of dealing with this is to assume that advertising is subject to the lagged effect common to all other independent variables plus a lagged effect of its own. This formulation can be handled by using a secondary Koyck transformation.[16] Another approach is to bring out explicitly the concept of advertising stock that is implicit in the Koyck treatment. The stock of advertising (interpretable as the stock of goodwill that has been built up by advertising) can be represented by some function of past and present levels of advertising. Unless information on the way in which advertising messages are received and forgotten and on the distribution of the effects of advertising over time is available, the formula for combining past and present levels of advertising into a stock measure has to be arrived at by experimenting to see which stock measure leads to the best degree of fit for the advertising effectiveness equation.

Simultaneous regression studies In estimating the effect of advertising expenditure on sales, the dependence of the advertising budget on past or expected sales levels may affect the relationship. Although within a given budget period an increase in sales beyond the budgeted level may not affect advertising in the same period, in some cases it will increase the budget for the following period. The problem of reverse causation is most likely to occur where the product or market is new to the firm and management is not sure how much to allocate to advertising because it has very little indication of effectiveness. In such cases, a resort to rules of thumb, such as allocating a proportion of sales revenue to advertising, is particularly likely. Even if there are substantial diseconomies of scale in the use of advertising, higher sales mean more to be defended, and management may increase advertising budgets irrespective of diseconomies. Given the above points, it is customary to estimate simultaneously an advertising effectiveness equation and an advertising budget equation.[17]

Using more or less standard demand functions, modified to take into account simultaneous relationships and lagged effects, a number of econometric studies of the effects of advertising on sales have been carried out.[18] These studies are of greatest practical use when applied to analysis of the optimality of advertising expenditure.

The optimal level of advertising Theoretically, the profit maximising firm will use each promotional method up to the point where its marginal revenue productivity equals its marginal cost. This simple marginal approach to promotional allocation is attractive, but needs to be applied with care in this context. The sales function relates revenue to price, promotional expenditure, income of buyer, and so on. The effect of some kinds of promotion is to reduce the elasticity of demand for a product (by increasing differentiation), thereby allowing the firm to achieve a higher price, while other kinds of promotion produce a market broadening, allowing a larger volume to be sold at the same price. In other words some methods rotate the demand curve while others shift it outwards. This implies that different kinds and amounts of promotional input change the effectiveness of the price 'input' into the sale process in different ways. Some promotional inputs may only be effective if price is changed, implying inflexibility in proportions in the sales function (parallel to fixed proportions in a production function). This kind of interdependence needs to be taken into account. Empirically, this means that studies of advertising effectiveness and optimality should include situations of significant price change.

The business aims of the firm have an important impact on advertising allocation. Consider the difference between the profit maximising firm and the firm aiming to maximise sales revenue subject to a profits constraint. The profit maximiser will allocate funds according to the standard marginal rule, with more funds going to any method where marginal revenue productivity exceeds marginal cost. The sales maximiser's behaviour is less predictable, depending on elasticities of demand with respect to price and promotion and on the elasticity of cost with respect to output. If promotion is highly productive and cheap and demand very price elastic and there are diseconomies of scale in production, the revenue maximiser will go for higher promotional levels than will the profit maximiser. Here, the revenue maximiser would be using up some of his profits by selling more units at marginal losses. But if promotion is highly ineffective and price elasticity of demand very low, but economies of scale (and hence diseconomies of low output) substantial, we should expect the revenue maximiser to use less promotion than the profit maximiser and set a high price, thereby using up profits by achieving a high revenue (but not physical) turnover at high cost. In other words, the sales maximiser may not use more of *all* sales increasing methods than the profit maximiser.[19]

As most firms probably have business aims falling between these two extremes, the implication of this point is that in making promotional allocation, management needs to take into account the interrelationship between promotion, price, output, costs and profits.[20] Given the complexity of the problem, it is interesting to note that some empirical studies support the contention that in some industries, advertising is close to the optimum for a profit maximising firm (more or less advertising would not increase profitability). One study found that on a year-to-year basis, advertising in non-durable goods industries was close to optimum, while for durables the divergence was considerable, advertising being considerably less than the optimum (given by the relationship between its cost and its revealed effectiveness).[21] One explanation of this might be that there is a higher chance (in durable rather than non-durable goods industries) that retaliation in advertising will be stronger and faster than retaliation in price (implying a reluctance to use advertising as opposed to other competitive weapons). Another possibility is that in durable goods industries estimates of the advertising elasticity of demand based on yearly data are exaggerated, either because one of the principal effects of advertising – especially when associated with the launch of new models – is to bring forward purchasing and not increase total demand,[22] or because bursts of advertising in durable goods industries tend to be strongly associated with bursts of other (unmeasured) promotional activity.

ECONOMICS AND THE PROMOTIONAL DECISION

Taking into account the analysis of previous chapters, we can say that an 'economic' approach to promotion needs to include the following stages:

1. Clarification of targets Management needs to clarify what profit, market share or other targets apply to the products for which promotional policy is being considered, taking into account the dependence of the targets themselves on assessments of the feasibility of policies that require promotional inputs (for analysis of promotion may show particular targets to be infeasible or to be too pessimistic).

2. Clarification of constraints, policy options, etc. The upper limits to promotional spending (overall and particular forms) need to be established and their rationale investigated, together with other policy options that may achieve the same effect (price, product line change, etc.) or may need to be used in conjunction with promotional policy.

3. Obtaining required information The information required depends on the method of analysis chosen. However, likely information requirements include the following:

(a) Physical sales volumes of the firm's products and of competing firms' products (individually if possible) for a number of past years (depending on reliability and comparability of data for more distant years);

(b) Prices of the firm's and competitors' products over the period selected for analysis;

(c) Promotional expenditures of all kinds, for all firms' products in the market (or, as a minimum, aggregate promotional expenditure);

(d) If products are differentiated, some measure of different product qualities or else some way of dividing the data such that products in different but related product classes can be treated separately;

(e) Measures of customers' capacity to buy (income, liquidity, turnover, etc.); and

(f) Measures of variables representing buyers' demand for product characteristics, from general factors (for example social and psychological) to specific product-related variables (the variables to be included depending on the nature of the product, buyer and competition and how far management wants to go in analysing the effectiveness of different components of the promotional mix).

4. Deciding the nature of the analysis to be carried out on the data Analyses which management might want to carry out include the following:

(a) Testing the effectiveness of different forms of promotion, given other elements of the marketing mix;

(b) Testing the effectiveness of promotion relative to other elements of the marketing mix;

(c) Testing how far promotional expenditure by the firm and its competitors has effects which cancel each other out or lead to genuine market expansion; and

(d) Testing the link between promotion and achievement of business aims.

5. Carrying out the chosen analysis Consider the above tests. Testing the effectiveness of different promotional forms within a given marketing policy framework could be dealt with at the level of purchasing behaviour–promotional expenditure analysis, using standard econometric techniques. A more comprehensive approach would be to attempt to account for changes in purchasing behaviour through looking at the effect of promotion on buyers' demand for product characteristics, perhaps by grouping buyers' preferences by clustering techniques and showing how changes in promotional mix affect clustering, followed by analysis of the relationship between clustering of preferences and purchasing.

The same general approach would be appropriate for analysing the effectiveness of promotion relative to other elements of the marketing mix, except that for computational purposes the different promotional variables might have to be condensed into a limited number of combined variables (possibly using factor analysis if there is some intercorrelation between usage of different promotional methods). At this stage the likely two-directional nature of the relationship between promotional expenditure and sales will need to be taken into account, while promotional variables will have a lagged effect relative to other marketing variables.

Cancelling-out may apply not only to promotion, but also to other policy variables. So the first step here is to test for covariation between the firm's promotional expenditure and each element of its competitors' marketing mix, taking into account lagged responses. Such testing may be undertaken by defining a response variable (a weighted combination of the elements of competitor's marketing mix) for each competitor. If competitors frequently respond to changes in promotion, it may be difficult to test for the effects of promotion when there is no cancelling out. If competitors retaliate automatically, the effectiveness of promotion may never be established. It is therefore important to identify periods where retaliation is limited. A policy implication of automatic responses coupled with limited promotional effectiveness may be that collusion is appropriate. At any rate this analysis may give an indication of what sort of responses are to be expected and what sort of actions a firm can take to force its competitors' hands.

Testing for the effectiveness of promotion in achieving the firm's business aims requires analysis of the costs of promotion and of the policies that accompany it (such as increased production to accompany a sales drive). From the analysis of the contribution of promotion to sales, estimates of the marginal revenue productivity of promotion can be obtained and compared with cost estimates. Note that promotional increases may be applied with or without accompanying changes in other elements of the marketing mix. Because it is not *a priori* possible to say which mix combination is best, several possibilities need to be set up for investigation. Note too that the element of competitive retaliation is likely to be important here. This may require treatment by simulation in the light of what is known about the effectiveness of different elements of the marketing mix and business aims of competitors.

Although the above kinds of analysis may seem extremely demanding of data, it is at any rate worth marketing management's while to consider how some aspects of the above approaches might be applied to promotional allocation decisions.

12 Distribution Policy

The use of third parties to convey or sell a firm's output to the final customer complicates the relationship between the firm and its markets. The distribution system that a firm uses affects the price that it can get, the quantity it can sell, the kinds of products it can sell, the promotional methods it needs to use, the kind and amount of information it can transmit to and receive from its customers, and so on. In short, the distribution system affects every aspect of marketing.

Distribution policy has its short and its long-term aspects. In the short term, management concerns include the prices that can be obtained, promotional policies, amount of produce sold and getting information to and from the customer, given the firm's existing distribution system. In the long term, management concerns include the feasibility of different distribution systems, the possibility of changing or modifying systems, how the system currently being used is evolving, what kinds of products can be sold through the firm's current or other distribution systems, how the evolution of competition in the firm's own industry and in the distribution system affects relationships between producers and distributors, and so on. Because of work pressures, marketing management may concentrate unduly on short-term policy issues. However, the long-run factors determine the context in which short-run policy issues need to be resolved and therefore merit equal attention.

In the marketing literature, distribution systems are partly analysed under the name 'marketing channels', a term that underlines the fact that the work of marketing to the final user is often shared between producers and distributors. Distribution is not simply an extension of producing firms but an industry in its own right. The distribution industry is in the same general marketing position as industries that produce a physical product. Most of the subject matter of the preceding chapters of this book can be applied to the distribution industries. Distributive firms succeed or fail according to whether they offer the right combination of product (in this case service, location, etc.) price and promotion. They have similar problems of demand forecasting (in this case concerning location of custom, type of service required and product variety demanded). Product planning (related to the service/location/product variety complex of factors) may be characterised by a lag of several years from plan to implementation, making demand forecasting more important than in many manufacturing firms. In this chapter the economics of distribution systems are not considered in detail.[1] The aim of this chapter is to pick out the factors that are most important in determining the nature of the relationship between producers and distributors.

The nature of this relationship depends on the following factors:

1. the proportion of the physical and commercial marketing process that is carried out by distributors;

2. the use and availability of technologies for carrying out distributive tasks;

3. the unit costs of inputs into the distributive process;

4. the nature of competition among firms to supply products through the distribution system to the final customer, among distributors at all levels (retail, wholesale etc.) to *obtain* the products produced by the competing group of firms, among distributors to *sell* the products, and among final customers to obtain the products;

5. customers' demand for distribution services and distributors' success in meeting these demands; and

6. legal, fiscal, financial or conventional restrictions on the working of the distribution system.

These are the principal economic-related factors. Note that most of them are interdependent. For example, competition among distributors to sell leads to faster evolution of distributive technologies, greater downward pressure on distributive costs and greater ease of marketing for manufacturing firms. Let us consider these factors in turn.

1. THE PROPORTION OF THE MARKETING PROCESS CARRIED OUT BY DISTRIBUTORS

Standard classifications of the functions which may, in whole or in part, be performed by distributors include transfer of ownership, transfer of physical possession, negotiation with the final customer, financing the purchase, promotion, holding stock, breaking bulk, selecting products, absorbing business risk, concentration of ordering, easing or creating flows of information between customer and manufacturer and provision of services associated with the use of the product. In choosing between distribution systems and in managing them, marketing management needs to evaluate which of these tasks the firm can do more efficiently and which less efficiently than existing distribution systems. Each task requires inputs which have a cost to the firm or to the distributor, a cost which will be reflected in the net price that the producer can obtain for his product. Sometimes it may be more profitable for the producing firm to do nearly all the work (as with many industrial products and services). In other cases (common in export marketing) the firm may use the services of distributive firms so extensively that well over half of the final price is made up of distributors' costs and profits. In principle marketing management should decide on the allocation of marketing tasks between the firm and distributive firms on the basis of a comparison of the opportunity costs of carrying out the tasks with the revenue forgone by paying distributive firms to do them. Analysis of the firm's own costs and those of existing modes of distribution may even show that it would pay the firm to set up its own distribution system in competition with existing distributors or encourage the emergence of new forms of distribution.

The total cost of carrying out marketing tasks depends mainly on the unit costs of the inputs required and on the technologies available (as these determine input combinations required for a given marketing output). Marketing management should therefore decide on the allocation of tasks between the firm and distributors according to the firm's comparative advantage (relative to distributors) in obtaining and using inputs and technologies. Let us explore this point through an example.

Suppose that the marketing manager of a canned grocery foods manufacturer is considering which marketing tasks his firm should perform and which should be delegated to distributors. Several of his major supermarket chain customers have moved to using regional warehouses for concentrating incoming goods. From these warehouses, deliveries to individual supermarkets are made in complete container loads, economising on the transport fleet and saving the individual supermarket considerable effort in scheduling and handling incoming loads. These customers are pressing the firm for lower delivered prices (which some competitors have already conceded). However, this change in physical distribution technology by customers has undermined the firm's own physical distribution technology, which was based on direct delivery to stores on the basis of carefully worked-out schedules in urban areas. Many customers still want direct deliveries, so marketing management has to consider how the change will affect the overall profitability of the existing system. Analysis of the costs of the reduced direct delivery system shows that the customers' move has made the firm's own physical distribution system completely unviable and that it would be better for the firm to suspend even more of the marketing operation by encouraging (through a change in the discount structure) all other distributors to order through wholesalers or take substantial deliveries. Distributors still requiring direct delivery would be served through common carriers.[2]

In economic terms, the change in customers' policy has reduced the size of the firm's own market for distributive services. The firm becomes less able to exploit economies of scale in physical distribution, so that the unit costs of physical distribution as supplied by the firm rise. The firm's relative advantage in carrying out this particular marketing task has disappeared; as a result it is forced to seek another technology. His customers are better placed to carry out the task of physical distribution (defined according to their requirements).

The implication of these changes for the firm's profitability depends partly on the efficiency of the system used previously. By disposing entirely of its transport fleet, concentrating deliveries to regional supermarket warehouses and to wholesalers, and using common carriers the firm's net return on capital may increase because the previous system tied up capital in a relatively inefficient use. This possibility emphasises the importance of calculating the true opportunity costs of inputs tied up in distribution work and comparing them with the cost of farming out distribution work.[3]

This point is further emphasised when we consider the impact of the distributional division of labour on other policy variables. For example, the proportion of the distribution process carried out by the manufacturer may affect the volume of sales that he can make. A firm which sells for export entirely through independent importing agents may be less well placed to identify gaps in market coverage (and hence make fewer sales) than a firm which runs its own foreign sales branches (this is not, of course, a sufficient reason for setting up wholly owned sales branches). In this case the firm needs to analyse the opportunity costs and benefits of employing market research, promotional and other inputs directly or through distributors.

Similar considerations may apply with respect to product variety. The greater the proportion of the distributive task carried out by the producer, the more control he may have over the nature and variety of products which can reach the final buyer and the better placed he may be to identify gaps in the product range. This does not imply that completely vertically integrated concerns will market a wider range of products. In fact it is arguable that because greater product variety brings heavier stock-holding costs (a large element in most distribution system costs), the more completely integrated firm is more likely to give this factor heavy weighting in product planning decisions.

The relationship of the overall division of labour between producer and distributor to the promotional division of labour is rather complex. Because distributors may be concerned only about their overall sales levels rather than the sales of any specific product, producers' promotion may have to concentrate on pulling products through the system. The less the producer's overall involvement in distribution, the harder he may have to promote to sell his products. At the same time, the greater the producer's direct involvement with final buyers, the more of the burden of general promotion he has to carry. In economic terms promotion is sometimes a complement and sometimes a substitute for distributional involvement of other kinds.[4]

2. THE USE AND AVAILABILITY OF TECHNOLOGIES FOR CARRYING OUT DISTRIBUTIVE TASKS

Technology – in the broad sense of 'ways of organising inputs' – is important in two general respects. Firstly it affects the relative efficiency of producer and distributor in carrying out particular distributive tasks. Secondly it affects the absolute cost of the distribution process.

RELATIVE POSITIONS OF PRODUCER AND DISTRIBUTOR

Consider the example of television advertising, which may substitute for the personal attention of an in-store sales assistant, for it allows the producer to address final customers in a more direct manner than printed advertising. This promotional technology led to some producers taking a much larger share of the promotional task and to an enhanced ability to control product variety and volume – and sometimes price. In some industries it led to distributors completely abandoning the promotion of particular products and encouraged distributive technologies to evolve away from personal in-store promotion.

ABSOLUTE COST OF THE DISTRIBUTIVE PROCESS

The evolution of distributive technologies does not necessarily imply a reduction in total distribution costs for given products. As incomes rise, customers may demand more convenient or pleasant ways of purchasing. The service proportion of purchases may increase and appropriate technologies may develop for the provision of extra service elements. At the same time, competition within the distributive trades will lead to a search for, and implementation of, new technologies which allow given distributive packages (location of products, conditions of purchase, variety of product) to be offered at a lower cost. Whether cost reductions are passed on (to the producer or the final buyer) depends on competitive structures.

Developments in distributional technology also affect product variety and sales volumes of each product. The use of television to show what products are available coupled with telephone ordering reduces the pressure on distributors to keep product variety down, for products do not have to be displayed in a retail location but may be shipped from a central warehouse. This may encourage the development of broader product ranges at producer level, with each product having a lower sales volume. This will also affect the structure of competition among producing firms, for it reduces competition among firms for shelf space and allows firms which might have suffered from such competition to survive more easily. This kind of development represents a reversal of previous trends in the development of technology which resulted from the search for cheaper methods of distribution. The development of self-service technology favoured high turnover products and helped eliminate lower turnover products, making some producers dependent on a small number of very high volume items.

3. THE UNIT COSTS OF INPUTS INTO THE DISTRIBUTIVE PROCESS

Movements in the costs of inputs into distribution may change the relations between the producer and the distributor as well as the structure of the distribution system itself. Let us consider examples from two of the basic cost categories:

Labour costs The effect of rising real labour costs is to cause distributors to substitute other inputs (for instance self-service selection space and higher stocks) for labour. The overall effect of the labour cost rise will be to raise the total cost of distribution, unless technological change, which the cost rise will encourage, creates systems which allow total input costs to be reduced. If the real cost of distribution then rises, the producer may – depending on the elasticity of final customer demand for distribution services and on the structure of distributional costs (for example whether there are economies of scale) and competition – need to reduce his demand for distribution services or seek less labour-intensive modes of distribution.

Capital costs In some countries as capital markets develop, there is a fall in the real price of funds for secure investments as a result of the market's enhanced ability to assess risk. Because investment in stocks of finished goods is less risky, there may be a fall in the cost of capital for distribution firms which, depending on competitive structures, may be passed on to producers. In such cases it may pay producers to transfer more stock-holding tasks to their distributors abroad. Differences in the cost of capital to producer and foreign distributor are often substantial in export marketing situations. Governments often subsidise capital required for exporting purposes and restrict capital (or increase its cost) for importing purposes. Such policies may influence the division of stock-holding and financing roles between producer and distributor.

4. THE NATURE OF COMPETITION AMONG FIRMS TO SUPPLY PRODUCTS, AMONG DISTRIBUTORS TO OBTAIN PRODUCTS, AMONG DISTRIBUTORS TO SELL PRODUCTS AND AMONG CUSTOMERS TO OBTAIN PRODUCTS

In this vertical arrangement of four competing systems (not to mention additional systems of competition within multi-layer distribution systems), the effect of each system depends on the behaviour of the other three systems. Each system may vary from the purely competitive to the monopolistic. This variation is not completely independent. For example, if national distribution is monopolised, this applies both to the distributor's obtaining and to his selling the product. Also, the characteristics of one system may set up pressures which lead to changes in other systems (for instance concentration in the distributive trades may produce concentration among suppliers, and vice versa).[5] The number of possible combinations of types of system is large, so here we shall consider some of the general determinants of the nature of interaction among competitive systems and their implications for marketing management.

Where all four competitive systems are perfectly competitive in the strictest theoretical sense, there is little role for marketing in the normal sense of the word. If there is a departure from this state in *one* of the systems, then we can still apply the standard theoretical models (monopolistic competition, oligopoly, monopoly, etc. and their counterparts in purchasing analysis), at least as the first stage of the analysis. Note that if an independent distribution system exists, then the distributive barrier to entry for producers is much weaker and this may moderate the behaviour of monopoly or oligopoly suppliers of products. Similarly, the possibility of circumventing powerful distributors in oligopsony situations may limit their market behaviour. In practice, however, distribution channels are characterised by imperfections in competition at more than one level.

With imperfections in competition at more than one level, any purely competitive system which performs a linking function between two imperfectly competitive systems will assume a role which has little significance for the commercial nature of the transaction between the two imperfectly competitive systems. Here, the intervening, perfectly competitive system can be seen as a straightforward input into the distribution process, performing a specific set of functions (for instance stock-holding or physical distribution). A good example of this is the physical distribution input supplied by common carriers.

Transactions among competing systems which are imperfectly competitive are likely to be based on bargaining among the parties concerned. The outcome of the bargaining will depend mainly on what might be called 'power' factors, although there will be limits to the outcome imposed by cost, revenue and profitability factors. The price governing transactions between producers and distributors will have an upper limit – determined partly by each distributor's estimate of the turnover of each product at different price levels, of the cost of holding stock, of the cost of selling the item, of the likelihood of other distributors being able to sell similar products at lower prices, and so on – and a lower limit – determined by each producer's estimate of turnover, costs and profitability for each product. There will therefore be a range of prices outside which either the producer or distributor prefers not to conclude the transaction. Similar forces will be at work in the areas of product variety (although here either the producer or the

distributor may want more or less variety), sales volumes and promotional levels.

Given these limits, there are several factors that need to be taken into
account in analysing bargaining of this kind.[6] Using X to represent the
typical producer and Y to represent the typical distributor, we can say
that X's degree of channel control (his ability to determine price, sales
volume, product variety and promotion, together with the general
evolution of channel structure, to his own satisfaction) depends upon
the following kinds of factors.[7]

(a) The strength of X's base of power relative to that of Y[8] This refers to
the *resources* that X can use to influence Y's behaviour and vice versa.
X's power base is determined by factors such as the franchise his product
has with the final buyer (brand image, etc.), his importance relative to his
competitors as a supplier of the product, his importance for Y as a
supplier of expert information,[9] the breadth and buoyancy of his
product mix, and his managerial resources, which determine his ability
to withstand adverse moves, such as refusal to stock, and to initiate
moves, such as forward integration into distribution. Y's power base is
determined by the strength of his franchise as a distributor (which
determines the volume of products he can sell and the exposure he can
give to existing and new products), his relative importance as a buyer of
the product and as a supplier of information to the producer, the
breadth and buoyancy of his product mix and his financial and
managerial resources.[10]

These points imply that it is important for marketing management to
attempt to build and maintain the firm's power base by, for example,
strengthening the franchise of the firm's products, increasing the degree
of diversification of the firm's product range, attempting to obtain a
larger market share by methods which do not (as price competition
does) involve making substantial concessions to distributors (perhaps
with a view to imposing a price leadership structure on the supplying
group of firms) and strengthening the managerial team which deals with
distribution policy. It is also important to build up the visibility and
credibility of the power base. This may be possible by concentrating on
promotion of the firm's complete product range under one brand name
(which might have the effect of increasing the impact of the absence of
the range from given outlets).

(b) The scope of X's means of power relative to Y's This refers to the
kinds of action that X can take to influence Y's behaviour and vice versa.

It concerns (on X's side) such actions as refusing or delaying supply[11] or fixing the price at which the distributor may sell,[12] fixing conditions of payment by the distributor and (on Y's side) refusing to stock, taking limited stocks, delaying payment, refusing to promote, and so on. The kinds of action that each channel member may take is partly determined by the way in which the channel is organised. Many channels are composed of more or less completely independent units; each performs its own function and co-ordinates its activities with other members of the channel solely through piecemeal bargaining, negotiation, and so on. In this type of system lack of co-ordination may reduce the system's efficiency below its potential. Each decision maker is concerned with costs, prices, profits, investment, etc. at his own stage of the marketing process. Decisions that he makes to increase his own profit may reduce the productivity of the whole system.[13] Some channel members may avoid the disadvantages of this kind of system by introducing an element of more stable co-ordination with their vertical counterparts. This may involve investment in helping them to make changes which are cost saving to both parties, or relinquishing the right to make changes which bring short-term profit gains to the individual firm (for example cancelling deals) at the expense of channel profitability.[14] The most effective co-ordination is likely to involve contractual arrangements, which provide the security necessary to obtain commitment to changes that may be required to increase overall channel efficiency.[15]

The type of restrictions that the producer accepts and the share he receives of the gains that may be made by achieving some degree of channel co-ordination will be determined partly by the bargaining power that he possesses in the first place. This in turn depends upon the kinds of action he would be able to take if there were no real co-ordination. In taking the initiative in increasing the degree of channel co-ordination, the producer needs to weigh the long-term gains that may be available from different types of channel co-ordination and the effects the co-ordination may have on limiting or promoting structural change in the channel.[16]

(c) *The set of Y's or X's over whom X or Y has power* This refers to the number of firms at the same level in the channel that X or Y 'dominates'. Selling to a large number of distributors differs from selling to a small number of distributors, in that in the latter case the distributors are likely to be able to maintain a stronger bargaining front. If having a large number of distributors implies that distributors will be smaller firms, then the producer's bargaining strength will be still greater. The

greater the number of distributors, the less the risks associated with cancellation of orders by any one distributor and the stronger the bargaining line that may be taken. However, these advantages have to be offset against the possible increased costs of order handling etc.

(d) The opportunity costs to each party of attempting to influence the other party, of being influenced by the other party (i.e. doing what the other party wants) and of resisting the influence of the other party (i.e. of bearing the sanctions that the other party may impose) The opportunity costs of policies (and of their consequences for other channel members) depend on the targets (aims, goals, etc.) which each channel member pursues. For example, the opportunity cost to the producer of retailer opposition to increased product variety is not only the profit forgone by lost sales of additional products but also the inability to achieve other targets (such as risk spreading). Targets (and hence opportunity costs) are likely to be adjusted on the basis of experience. Therefore, a constructive approach to exploiting another channel member's susceptibility to opportunity cost pressure stemming from the firm's policies is to use that pressure to work towards a change in the channel member's targets so that they are more consonant with those of the firm. For example, a producer may be sales growth oriented while its distributors prefer the status quo. In order to achieve its growth aims, the firm may threaten to use other distributors and at the same time attempt to persuade its current distributors of the advantage of growth. If, on the other hand, the producer finds himself in a weak bargaining position, it may be better for him to make his own targets more consonant with those of his distributors in order to reduce the chances that his policies will come into conflict with those of his distributors (leading to his incurring the costs of the conflict).

Conflict (the basic source of opportunity costs being incurred in this context) arises from various sources, such as target incompatibility, role conflict (for instance when a manufacturer carries out some distribution functions in competition with his own distributors), divergent assessments of reality (for instance when a producer disagrees with his distributors about the chances of success for a new product – note that this type of conflict may arise from communication problems) and perceived imbalance in the relationship between rewards and contribution.[17] It is not necessarily appropriate for the producer to attempt to avoid conflict and its associated opportunity costs completely. Conflict may be exploited constructively. This may be done by threatening (but rarely using) policies which impose substantial opportunity costs on distributors while ensuring that the overall relationship improves through policies which contain benefits to distributors which are relatively costless to the firm.

(e) The extent to which other X's and Y's co-operate with the X and the Y involved in the bargaining Because the competing group of X's normally have some common interest in their dealings with the Y's, it may be possible to restrain competition or increase co-operation among the X's in order to reduce the bargaining power of the Y's over the X's. The long-run advantages of co-operation for the individual firm depends on its efficiency (in the widest sense of the term) relative to the firms with which it co-operates. If a firm is relatively very efficient, its best long-term strategy may be to create temporary bargaining weakness throughout the level of competition at which it operates by engaging in intense competition with other firms and only later adopting a leadership strategy (for what may be a reduced number of competitors).

Attempts to co-operate may be hampered by organisational and legal factors. Producers' attempts to co-operate in bargaining against strong distributors may be susceptible to defection if distributors are able to exploit differences among producers. This may be done by offering to make special arrangements for the promotion of the products of one producer in exchange for special discounts. Legal restrictions on co-operation among producers vary among countries. The kinds of policy on which restrictions are commonly in force include refusal to supply, resale price maintenance and discrimination in territorial allocations of produce.[18]

EFFECTS OF BARGAINING POWER ON THE STRUCTURE OF COMPETITION

As well as affecting the short-run aspects of marketing, the nature of competitive bargaining among channel members may lead to structural changes in the different competing systems. Suppose that an oligopoly of producers is faced with an oligopsony of distributors. The outcome of bargaining on product variety will be that the least profitable goods to produce will be eliminated, as will the products which are the less profitable for distributors to stock. The products eliminated on each side are unlikely to be identical, for production elimination will occur partly because the products cannot exploit the production resources, experience, etc. of the producers, while distribution elimination will occur partly because of lack of enough overlap in market with other products stocked. In this situation there may be a substantial amount of frustrated final buyer demand (demand for products outside the range on offer). This may lead to a search for technologies of production and distribution to enable this demand to be met, a search which need not necessarily be undertaken by existing firms in the competing group. If the search is successful, it may lead to the development of more intensive competition at producer or distributor levels. In addition the 'gap' opened up by the bargaining groups policies may be exploitable by, say, smaller companies operating with different (not new) production or distributive technologies.

This example brings out the general point that competition among firms at all levels in marketing channels takes place in the context of changing input costs, technologies and final demand. The major long-run determinant of success for firms in any of the competing systems is ability to exploit new technologies, cheaper inputs and a failing of competitors to meet the changing demand for products and distributive services.

5. CUSTOMER DEMAND FOR DISTRIBUTION SERVICES

Distribution services, as we have seen, are a product in their own right, a product for which customers have a separate demand. These services may be provided by the producer or by distributive firms. As customers' demand for distributive services changes relative to their demand for the product itself, this may produce changes in the division of labour between producer and distributor, together with a change in marketing policies and in the gains from the transaction. Changes in the structure of demand for distributive services may relate to factors such as price range, product variety and purchase-associated services. As the demand mix changes, so new (sometimes parallel) distribution systems may arise. It is therefore important for the producer to check that the distribution systems he is using keep pace with changes in the demand for distributive services.

6. RESTRICTIONS ON THE WORKING OF THE DISTRIBUTION SYSTEM

As we have seen, legal restrictions affect the nature of the competitive relationship among members of distribution channels by fixing directly standards for the conduct of these relationships. More general policies (such as taxation rates on particular forms of sale) also affect channel relationships. For example, in some countries businesses below a certain size are exempt from value-added or turnover tax. This enables some of the smallest retailers to overcome cost disadvantages and to stay in the market, giving producers a wider choice of modes of distribution than if all retailers were treated alike.

THE MARKETING MANAGER AND THE DISTRIBUTION SYSTEM

In this chapter we have considered some aspects of producer–distributor relationships. In analysis and decisions on distribution policy and strategy, marketing management should treat the distribution system as a variable which is subject to considerable change over the long-term and which the firm itself can influence significantly.

Notes

CHAPTER 2

1. For a summary of economic analyses of business aims, see J. F. Pickering, *Industrial Structure and Market Conduct* (London, 1974) Chapter 6.
2. To the extent that the managing director of a firm reports to the chairman (if he is not one and the same person) and to his board, this is also true of private enterprise. Note that in some countries the board is responsible not to the shareholders but to the company, in the interests of which they are legally required to act.
3. For further discussion of these points, see R. M. Cyert and J. G. March, *A Behavioural Theory of the Firm* (Englewood Cliffs, N.J., 1963); O. E. Williamson, *The Economics of Discretionary Behaviour* (Englewood Cliffs, N.J., 1964); and R. L. Marris, *The Economic Theory of Managerial Capitalism* (London, 1964). For a summary of most of the main theses on this topic, see J. R. Wildsmith, *Managerial Theories of the Firm* (London, 1973).
4. Cyert and March, op. cit.
5. Trade-off may be established by a variety of statistical methods, including discriminant analysis of choices and conjoint analysis. For a discussion of the issues involved in using conjoint analysis, see I. Fenwick, 'A User's Guide to Conjoint Measurement in Marketing', *European Journal of Marketing* 12 (1978) pp. 203–11.
6. For a summary discussion of barriers to entry, see Pickering, op. cit., Chapter 4.
7. See J. A. Schumpeter, *The Theory of Economic Development* (Cambridge, Mass., 1934) and J. Downie, *The Competitive Process* (London, 1958) for theory and evidence on this point.
8. See H. M. Mann, 'Seller Concentration, Barriers to Entry and Rates of Return in 30 Industries, 1950–1960', *Review of Economics and Statistics* 48 (1966) pp. 291–307 and N. R. Collins and L. E. Preston, *Concentration and Price – Cost Margins in Manufacturing Industries* (University of California Press, 1968). Mann finds evidence that industries can be split into two groups, concentrated and unconcentrated; the former show significantly higher profitability than the latter, while intra-group differences in profitability are low. Collins and Preston suggest that the relationship is more continuous.
9. See K. D. George, *Industrial Organisation* (London, 1971) Chapter 6.
10. See, for example, M. N. Baily, 'Research and Development Costs and Returns in the US Pharmaceutical Industry', *Journal of Political Economy*

80 (1972) pp. 70–85; E. Mansfield, *Industrial Research and Technological Innovation, an Econometric Analysis* (New York, 1968); and W. J. J. Smith and D. Creamer, *R and D and Small Company Growth: A Statistical Review and Company Case Studies* (New York, for the National Industrial Conference Board, 1968).

11. Hence the 'kinked demand curve' theoretical solution, which explains why price may be slow to move in such situations, despite cost changes. For a discussion of the evidence on this and related issues, see Pickering, op. cit., Chapter 14.

12. See I. Horowitz, 'Research Inclinations of a Cournot Oligopolist', *Review of Economic Studies* 30 (1963) pp. 128–30 and F. M. Scherer, 'Research and Development Allocation under Rivalry', *Quarterly Journal of Economics* 81 (1967) pp. 359–94, for examples of theoretical analysis of this situation.

13. See, for example, W. L. Baldwin and G. L. Childs, 'The Fast Second and Rivalry in Research and Development', *Southern Economic Journal* 31 (1969) pp. 18–24.

14. See Schumpeter, op. cit.

15. Downie, op. cit.

16. H. I. Ansoff and J. Stewart, 'Strategies for a Technology-based Business', *Harvard Business Review*, November–December 1967.

17. See A. D. H. Kaplan, *Big Enterprise in a Competitive System* (Brooking, 1954) and G. Whittington, 'Changes in the Top 100 Quoted Manufacturing Companies in the United Kingdom 1948 to 1968', *Journal of Industrial Economics* 21 (1973) pp. 17–34.

18. See, for example, W. D. Hoffmann, 'Market Structure and Strategies of R & D Behaviour in the Data Processing Market – Theoretical Thoughts and Empirical Findings', *Research Policy* 5 (1976) pp. 334–53.

CHAPTER 3

1. See, for example, J. Bridge and J. C. Dodds, *Managerial Decision Making* (London, 1975) Chapters 1 and 2.

2. For a good brief description of the use of Lagrangean multipliers, see W. J. Baumol, *Economic Theory and Operations Analysis* (Englewood Cliffs, N.J., 2nd edn, 1965, pp. 60–5.

3. G. L. S. Shackle, *Uncertainty in Economics and Other Reflections* (Cambridge, 1955).

4. See L. Hurwicz, *Optimality criteria for decision making under ignorance*, Cowles Commission Discussion Paper, Statistics, No. 370, 1951, for further analysis of this point.

5. L. J. Savage, 'The Theory of Statistical Decision', *Journal of the American Statistical Association* 46 (1951) pp. 55–67.

6. See W. J. Abernathy, 'Some Issues Concerning the Effectiveness of Parallel Strategies in R & D Projects', *IEEE Transactions on Engineering Management*, EM-18 (1971) pp. 80–9.

CHAPTER 4

1. The balance of payments is strictly a true balance. Applying the terms 'deficit' or 'surplus' to the balance of payments is a loose way of referring to total trade and financial flows before taking into account transfers to or from the country's foreign exchange reserves.
2. See C. Saunders, *Engineering in Britain, West Germany and France: Some Statistical Comparisons* (Sussex European Research Centre, University of Sussex, Brighton, 1978).
3. The measures, all in index form, include the net barter terms of trade (an index of export prices divided by an index of import prices), the gross barter terms of trade (an index of export prices divided by an index of import quantity), single factoral terms of trade (net barter index adjusted for productivity changes in export-producing industries) and double factoral terms of trade (net barter index adjusted for productivity changes in industries producing a country's exports and its imports). Each measure focusses on a different aspect of the gains from trade.
4. For a good summary of the debate on this point, see M. O. Clement, R. L. Pfister and K. J. Rothwell, *Theoretical Issues in International Economics* (London, 1967) pp. 158–66.
5. See, for example, P. Streeten, 'Common Fallacies about the Common Market', *Weltwirtschaftliches Archiv* 90 (1963). For a summary of the issues, see Clement et al., op. cit., Chapter 4.
6. A good text for this is M. K. Evans, *Macroeconomic Activity: Theory, Forecasting and Control* (New York, 1969).
7. See, for example, R. Goldsmith, *A Study of Saving in the United States*, Vol. 1 (Princeton, N.J., 1955) p. 22.
8. J. S. Duesenberry, *Income, Saving and the Theory of Consumer Behaviour* (Cambridge, Mass., revised edn, 1967). Duesenberry also hypothesised that a ratchet effect might operate. A rise in income would lead to a corresponding rise in consumption expenditure, but a fall in income would not produce a fall in consumption expenditure. This has implications for demand in different product markets in times of fluctuating income.
9. For an example of the kinds of changes that can take place in relative incomes within quite short periods, see C. Saunders et al., *Winners and Losers: Pay Patterns in the 1970's* (Political and Economic Planning Broadsheet Vol. XLIII No. 570, London, 1977).
10. T. M. Brown, 'Habit Persistence and Lags in Consumer Behaviour', *Econometrica* 20 (1952) pp. 355–71.
11. M. Friedman, *A Theory of the Consumption Function* (Princeton, N.J., 1957).
12. There have been a number of empirical tests of the permanent income hypothesis. The evidence is mixed. For a summary of some of the evidence, see Evans, op. cit., pp. 19–34.
13. See J. Fisher, 'Consumer Durable Goods Expenditures, with Major Emphasis on the Role of Assets, Credit and Intentions', *Journal of the American Statistical Association* 58 (1963) p. 654. Fisher found that three-quarters of the explained variance that distinguished the group of consumers using credit to purchase a particular durable from the group using

cash was explained by whether or not the consumer had used credit previously. Fisher also found that those consumers with instalment debt outstanding were far more likely to use credit than those with no instalment debt outstanding. M. L. Lee, in 'An Analysis of Instalment Borrowing by Durable Goods Buyers', *Econometrica* 30 (1962) p. 781, found that given the decision to purchase, consumers with higher levels of outstanding debt were more likely to borrow to pay for the purchase.

14. See D. Patinkin, *Money, Interest and Prices* (New York, 2nd edn, 1965) Appendix M, for a list of consumption functions with liquid assets terms.

15. F. Modigliani and A. Ando, 'The "Life Cycle" Hypothesis of Saving: Aggregate Implications and Tests', *American Economic Review* 53 (1963) pp. 55–84.

16. See, for example, G. Katona, *Psychological Analysis of Consumer Behaviour* (New York, 1951) and E. Mueller, 'Effects of Consumer Attitudes on Purchases', *American Economic Review* 47 (1957) pp. 946–65. G. Katona, B. Strumpel and E. Zahn, in *Aspirations and Influence: Comparative Studies in the United States and Western Europe* (New York, 1971), suggest that the fact that savings ratios are higher in Western Europe than in the United States may be due to the observed pessimism of Western Europeans concerning the continuation of improvement in their financial situation. This also supports the Modigliani hypothesis of saving for a time when income might be lower. For a recent analysis of the effects of expectations (amongst other variables) on durables purchasing, see J. F. Pickering, 'The Durable Purchase Behaviour of the Individual Household', *European Journal of Marketing* 12 (1978) pp. 178–93

17. It is arguable that attitudes are highly dependent on the current state of the economy. F. G. Adams and E. W. Green, in 'Explaining and Predicting Aggregative Consumer Attitudes', *International Economic Review* 6 (1965) p. 281, find that 85 per cent of the variance in the attitudes index used by the University of Michigan Survey Research Centre (one of the pioneers in the use of attitude indices) was explained by per capita disposable income, length of the work week and net accessions (extra workers taken on) minus lay offs.

18. This is the assumption made in the initial presentation of the accelerator model by J. M. Clark, in 'Business Acceleration and the Law of Demand'. *Journal of Political Economy* 25 (1917) pp. 217–35.

19. On the question of the lag between the decision to invest and the actual investment expenditure, see S. Almon, 'The Distributed Lag between Capital Appropriations and Expenditures', *Econometrica* 33 (1965) pp. 178–96, and T. Mayer and S. Sonenblum, 'Lead Times for Fixed Investment', *Review of Economics and Statistics* 37 (1955) pp. 300–4. On the role of anticipations, see R. M. Sachs and A. G. Hart, 'Anticipations and Investment Behaviour: an Econometric Study of Quarterly Time Series for Large Firms in Durable Good Manufacturing' in *Determinants of Investment Behaviour* (New York, 1967) pp. 489–536.

20. For treatment of lags, see L. M. Koyck, *Distributed Lags and Investment Analysis* (Amsterdam, 1954).

21. For empirical tests of the accelerator principle, see J. R. Meyer and E. Kuh, 'Acceleration and Related Theories of Investment: an Empirical Enquiry',

Review of Economics and Statistics 37 (1955) pp. 217–30.

22. Keynesian analysis is in terms of the internal rate of return (the 'marginal efficiency of investment' – see J. M. Keynes, *General Theory of Employment, Interest and Money* (New York, 1936) p. 135.

23. See, for example, W. H. White, 'Interest Inelasticity of Investment Demand – the Case for Business Attitude Surveys Re-examined', *American Economic Review* 46 (1956) pp. 565–87.

24. See M. K. Evans and E. W. Green, 'The Relative Efficacy of Investment Anticipations', *Journal of the American Statistical Association* 61 (1966) pp. 104–16.

25. See M. Foss and V. Natrella, 'Investment Plans and Realisation – Reasons for Differences in Individual Cases', *Survey of Current Business* 37 (1957).

26. See R. W. Resek, 'Investment by Manufacturing Firms: a Quarterly Time Series Analysis of Industry Data', *Review of Economics and Statistics* 48 (1966) pp. 322–33.

27. See L. R. Klein and J. Popkin, 'An Econometric Analysis of the Postwar Relations between Inventory Fluctuations and Aggregate Economic Activity', Part III of *Inventory Fluctuations and Economic Stability* (Washington, 1961) pp. 71–86.

28. See for example, M. Lovell, 'Determinants of Inventory Investment' in E. F. Denison and L. R. Klein (eds.), *Models of Income Determination* (Princeton, N.J., 1964).

29. See, for example, J. C. R. Dow, *The Management of the British Economy* (London, 1964) and S. Brittan, *Steering the Economy* (Harmondsworth, Middlesex, revised edn, 1971) for analysis of the effects of policy on economic stability.

CHAPTER 5

1. For a summary of this technique, see W. J. Baumol, *Economic Theory and Operations Analysis* (Englewood Cliffs, N.J., 2nd edn, 1965) Chapter 20. For a full treatment, see H. B. Chenery and P. G. Clark, *Interindustry Economics* (New York, 1959).

2. For the application of this approach to the foundations of economic demand analysis, see K. Lancaster, 'A New Approach to Consumer Theory', *Journal of Political Economy* 84 (1966) pp. 132–57 and his 'Change and Innovation in the Technology of Consumption', *American Economic Review* Proceedings 56 (1966) pp. 14–23. This work is further refined in his book *Consumer Demand, A New Approach* (New York, 1971). For some criticisms of his approach, see R. Hendler, 'Lancaster's new approach to consumer demand and its limitations', *American Economic Review* 65 (1975) pp. 194–9.

3. For an example of this kind of technique in use, see V. Stefflre, 'Market Structure Studies: New Products for Old Markets and New Markets for Old Products', in F. Bass et al., *Application of the Behavioural Sciences in Marketing* (New York, 1968) pp. 251–68.

4. For a fuller discussion of this approach, see J. M. Heineke, *Microeconomics for Business Decisions* (Englewood Cliffs, N.J., 1976) Chapter 2.

5. For a summary of technological forecasting methods, see R. Coenen, 'The Use of Technological Forecasts in Government Planning', *Research Policy* 1 (1971) pp. 156–72; for use in small companies, see A. V. Bruno et al., 'Technological Forecasting in Small Companies', *Sloan Management Review* 15 (1973) pp. 49–63.

6. For views on the origin of technological change, see *Technology in Retrospect and Critical Events in Science*, Illinois Institute of Technology Research Institute (National Science Foundation, Washington, D.C., 1968).

7. For a study of the factors affecting the diffusion of industrial products, see L. Nabseth and G. F. Ray, *The Diffusion of New Industrial Processes: an International Study* (Cambridge, 1974).

CHAPTER 6

1. For theoretical analysis of this point, see J. E. Meade, 'The Optimal Balance between Economies of Scale and Variety of Products', *Economica* 41 (1974) pp. 359–67.

2 For an analysis of the relationship between production method and organisational form, see J. Woodward, *Industrial Organisation, Theory and Practice* (London, 1965) and D. J. Hickson et al., 'Operations Technology and Organisation Structure: an Empirical Reappraisal', *Administrative Science Quarterly* 14 (1969) pp. 378–97.

3. See K. J. Arrow, 'The Economic Implications of Learning by Doing', *Review of Economic Studies* 29 (1962) pp. 155–73, for a discussion of the general economic issues involved here.

4. See W. B. Hirschman, 'Profit from the Learning Curve', *Harvard Business Review*, January–February 1964, p. 125 and W. J. Abernathy and K. Wayne, 'Limits of the Learning Curve', *Harvard Business Review*, September–October 1974, pp. 109–19.

5. See 'New Slices for Kaiser's Melon', *Business Week*, 4 March 1967, pp. 149–50, for an example of how a payments scheme was devised to share the benefits of learning.

6. See R. E. Walton, 'How to Counter Alienation in the Plant', *Harvard Business Review*, November–December 1972, for examples of schemes which help to increase the application of learning, either indirectly (because they produce greater workforce stability) or directly (because they allow for immediate transformation of learning into increased productivity).

7. See J. E. Tilton, *International Diffusion of Technology: the Case of Semiconductors* (Brookings, Washington, D.C., 1971) for a description of how the experience effect works in relation to production technology. See S. Hollander, *The Sources of Increased Efficiency: A Study of Du Pont Rayon Plants* (Cambridge, Mass., 1965) for an example of how costs are reduced by process improvements.

8. See Boston Consulting Group, *Perspectives in Experience* (Boston, Mass., 1972) for the suggestion that trade-offs between such major input elements as research and development and advertising can be a major source of

saving, as more is learnt about the determinants of success for particular products.

9. See BETRO Trust, *Concentration on Key Markets* (London, 3rd edn, 1977) for an analysis of the arguments for and against specialisation. This topic is also considered in Chapter 9.

10. For several examples of this, see C. Layton, Y. S. Hu and M. Whitehead, *Industry and Europe* (Political and Economic Planning, London, 1971).

11. See, for example, J. R. Moroney, 'Cobb Douglas Production Functions and Returns to Scale in U.S. Manufacturing Industry', *Western Economic Journal* 6 (1967) pp. 39–51. This study confirms the existence of constant returns to scale over a wide range of output levels. For more general discussion of the problems of statistical cost estimation, see A. A. Walters, 'Production and Cost Functions', *Econometrica* 31 (1963) pp. 1–66 (this contains a good summary of research findings) and J. Johnston, *Statistical Cost Analysis* (New York, 1960). For a multi-product analysis, see R. S. Koot and D. A. Walker, 'Short Run Cost Functions of a Multiproduct Firm', *Journal of Industrial Economics* 18 (1970) pp. 118–28.

12. For example, A. A. Thompson, Jr., in *Economics of the Firm: Theory and Practice* (Englewood Cliffs, N.J., 2nd edn, 1977) p. 287, cites the result of the McGraw-Hill annual survey of manufacturing firms that preferred rates of operation range in the neighbourhood of 90 per cent of the capacity rate as evidence that higher rates of production would entail increased manufacturing costs. There may be other reasons for this response on the part of managers. First, very high rates of production produce increased tension and stress and managers therefore prefer to keep a margin of safety. Second, preferred operational rates may be based on minimum marginal cost rather than minimum average cost.

13. See Walters, op. cit.

CHAPTER 7

1. For in-depth analysis, see D. A. Aaker, *Multivariate Analysis in Marketing: Theory and Application* (Belmont, California, 1971) and P. E. Green and J. D. Carrol, *Analysing Multivariate Data* (New York, 1978).

2. For practical advice on economy in the number of variables as a way of reducing problems of this kind, see G. Yule and M. G. Kendall, *An Introduction to the Theory of Statistics* (London, 14th edn, 1958) Chapter 13.

3. For the basic theory of canonical correlation, see Harold Hotelling, 'Relations between two sets of variables', *Biometrica* 28 (1936) pp. 321–77.

4. For a discussion of the connections between these two methods, see M. G. Kendall, *A Course in Multivariate Analysis* (London, 1961) Chapter 2.

5. For example, a questionnaire study might have asked consumers to indicate the likeliness (on a scale 1 to 5) of their purchasing 50 particular products over the next year. Factor analysis might show that high likelihood of buying wallpaper (WP) was correlated with high likelihood of buying paint (P), working tools (WT) and wood (W), with loadings of 0.8, 0.7, 0.5, and

0.3 respectively. This factor $(0.8WP + 0.7P + 0.5WT + 0.3W)$ might be called 'homemaker'.

6. The exception to this is where factor analysis has been used to reduce problems of multicollinearity.

7. This is done by hypothesising an equation for the line or plane, working out expressions for the sum of the squared deviations of the observations from the hypothesised line or plane, and using calculus to minimise the sum with respect to the coefficients of the hypothetical equation.

8. A lagged response might be represented as follows:

$$Y_t = b_0 X_t + b_1 X_{t-1} + b_2 X_{t-2} + \ldots + u_t \text{ (error term)}$$

where each of b's may have a value which is unrelated to that of any of the other b's. Estimation of such an equation is likely to be dogged by problems of multicollinearity among the X values in different time periods. If we make the simplest assumption, that the coefficients b are of exponentially declining importance, with weights w indicating this, then we can write

$$Y_t = bX_t + bwX_{t-1} + bw^2 X_{t-2} + \ldots u_t$$

Multiplying this expression by w and subtracting it from the expression for Y_{t+1}, we get

$$Y_{t+1} = w Y_t + bX_{t+1} + (u_{t+1} - wu_t)$$

Substituting for Y_{t+1} the expression $Y_t + \Delta Y_t$, we can obtain an expression which will overcome the multicollinearity problem, although we will still have problems with autocorrelation of the error terms.

For further discussion of lags, see L. M. Koyck, *Distributed Lags and Investment Analysis* (Amsterdam, 1954) and L. R. Klein, 'The estimation of distributed lags', *Econometrica* 26, (1958) pp. 553–65.

9. For more on this, see J. Johnston, *Econometric Methods* (New York, 1963) Chapter 9.

10. For more on functional forms and related aspects of cost functions, see J. M. Heineke, *Microeconomics for Business Decisions* (Englewood Cliffs, N.J., 1976) pp. 156–61. For some examples of more complicated forms used in diffusion analysis, see K. Brockhoff, 'A Test for the Product Life Cycle', *Econometrica* 35 (1967) pp. 472–84 and D. F. Midgley, *Innovation and New Product Marketing* (London, 1977) Chapter 5 ('Mathematical Theories of the Social Process').

11. For an application of discriminant analysis to explanation of mortgage debt, see G. H. Orcutt, M. Greenberger, J. Korbel and A. M. Revlin, *Microanalysis of Socioeconomic Systems: A Simulation Study* (New York, 1966) Chapter 12. For a general discussion of the interpretation of discriminant analysis, see D. G. Morrison, 'On the Interpretation of Discriminant Analysis', *Journal of Marketing Research* 6 (1969) pp. 159–63.

12. For an introduction to clustering methods, see R. E. Frank and P. E. Green, 'Numerical Taxonomy in Marketing Analysis: A Review Article', *Journal of Marketing Research* 5 (1968) pp. 83–98. For a more general discussion of

multidimensional techniques, see P. E. Green, 'Multidimensional Scaling: an Introduction and Comparison of Nonmetric Unfolding Techniques', *Journal of Marketing Research* 6 (1969) pp. 330–41.

CHAPTER 8

1. See H. I. Ansoff, 'Strategies for a Technology-based Business', *Harvard Business Review*, November–December 1967.
2. J. M. Blair, *Economic Concentration: Structure, Behaviour and Public Policy* (New York, 1972) pp. 201–4, reports Novick's finding that jumps in reported R and D spending without commensurate increases in R and D activity may be due to tax legislation or to 'fashions' in classifying activities.
3. See, for example, F. M. Scherer, 'Firm Size, Market Structure, Opportunity and the Output of Patented Inventions', *American Economic Review* 55 (1965) pp. 1097–1125; J. Schmookler, *Invention and Economic Growth* (Cambridge, Mass., 1966); W. S. Comanor and F. M. Scherer, 'Patent Statistics as a Measure of Technical Change'; *Journal of Political Economy*, 77 (1969) pp. 392–8; W. S. Comanor, 'Research and Technical Change in the Pharmaceutical Industry', *Review of Economics and Statistics* 47 (1965) pp. 182–90; E. Mansfield, *Industrial Research and Technological Innovation, an Econometric Analysis* (New York, 1968); and K. Pavitt and S. Wald, *The Conditions for Success in Technological Innovation* (Paris, OECD, 1971).
4. M. Gibbons and R. Johnston's 'The Roles of Science in Technological Innovation', *Research Policy* 3 (1974) pp. 220–42, gives an analysis of the relationship between science and innovation. A key finding is that the research results published in the scientific literature are used as information inputs into innovations on average about twelve years after publication. The use of scientific knowledge also depends crucially on the nature (ability and level of scientific education) of R and D staff.
5. See A. Phillips, 'Patents, Potential Competition and Technical Progress', *American Economic Review* (Part II Supplement) 56 (1966) pp. 301–10 and Scherer, op. cit.
6. See W. S. Comanor, 'Market Structure, Product Differentiation and Industrial Research', *Quarterly Journal of Economics* 81 (1967) pp. 639–57.
7. See J. Schmookler, *Invention and Economic Growth* (Cambridge, Mass., 1966) for a view that technological opportunity is of little importance compared with these factors.
8. See Comanor (1965) op. cit.; Scherer, op. cit.; A. S. Angilley, 'Returns to Scale in the Ethical Pharmaceutical Industry: Some Further Empirical Evidence', *Journal of Industrial Economics* 22 (1973) pp. 81–93; J. Schmookler, 'The Size of Firm and the Growth of Knowledge' in Z. Griliches and L. Hurwicz (eds.), *Patents, Invention and Economic Change* (Cambridge, Mass., 1972).
9. See A. C. Cooper, 'R and D is more efficient in small companies', *Harvard Business Review*, May–June 1964, pp. 75–83; Blair, op. cit.; and D. Hamberg, *R and D: Essays in the Economics of Research and Development* (New York, 1966).
10. See Pavitt and Wald, op. cit.

NOTES 167

11. See E. Mansfield, J. Rapoport, J. Schnee, S. Wagner and M. Hamburger, *Research and Innovation in the Modern Corporation* (New York, 1971).
12. See R. Rothwell et al., 'SAPPHO updated–Project SAPPHO Phase II', *Research Policy* 3 (1974) pp. 258–91.
13. For a summary of the effects of these processes, see D. Midgley, *Innovation and New Product Marketing* (London, 1977) Chapter 4.
14. W. R. Maclaurin, 'Technological Progress in Some American Industries', *American Economic Review* 44 (1954) pp. 178–89.
15. See I. Horowitz, 'Firm Size and Research Activity', *Southern Economic Journal* 28 (1962) pp. 298–301; Hamberg, op. cit.; and J. S. Worley, 'Industrial Research and the New Competition', *Journal of Political Economy*, 69 (1961) pp. 183–6.
16. F. M. Scherer, 'Market Structure and the Employment of Scientists and Engineers', *American Economic Review* 57 (1967) pp. 524–31.
17. See Comanor (1967) op. cit., for support for this point.
18. Ibid.
19. See D. C. Mueller and J. C. Tilton, 'Research and Development Costs as a Barrier to Entry', *Canadian Journal of Economics* 2 (1969) pp. 570–9.
20. See H. G. Grabowski and N. D. Baxter, 'Rivalry in Industrial Research and Development', *Journal of Industrial Economics* 21 (1973) pp. 209–35; I. Horowitz, 'Research Inclinations of a Cournot Oligopolist', *Review of Economic Studies* 30 (1963) pp. 128–30; and F. M. Scherer, 'Research and Development Allocation under Rivalry', *Quarterly Journal of Economics* 81 (1967) pp. 359–94, for further discussion of this point.
21. See Grabowski and Baxter, op. cit., Scherer (1965) op. cit. and Comanor (1965) op. cit.
22. J. A. Schumpeter, *The Theory of Economic Development* (Cambridge, Mass., 1934).
23. J. Downie, *The Competitive Process* (London, 1958).
24. Mansfield, op. cit.
25. E. T. Penrose, *The Theory of the Growth of the Firm* (Oxford, 1959).
26. For a wider discussion of the trade-off between product and market decisions, see W. R. Smith, 'Product Differentiation and Market Segmentation as Alternative Marketing Strategies', *Journal of Marketing* 21 (1956) pp. 3–8.
27. L. Abbott, *Quality and Competition* (New York, 1955).
28. See, for example, M. Freimer and L. S. Simon, 'The Evaluation of Potential New Product Alternatives', *Management Science* 13 (1967) pp. 279–92; H. J. Claycamp and L. E. Liddy, 'Prediction of New Product Performance: an Analytical Approach', *Journal of Marketing Research* 6 (1969) pp. 414–20; B. Inso, 'Concept Testing: an Appropriate Approach', *Journal of Marketing Research* 12 (1975) pp. 228–31; L. Light and L. Pringle, 'New Product Forecasting using Recursive Regression' in D. T. Kollat, R. D. Blackwell and J. F. Engel (eds.), *Research in Consumer Behaviour* (New York, 1970); W. F. Massy, 'Forecasting the Demand for New Convenience Products', *Journal of Marketing Research* 6 (1969) pp. 405–12; and Y. Wind, 'A New Procedure for Concept Evaluation', *Journal of Marketing* 37 (1973) pp. 2–11.

29. See, for example, W. J. Abernathy, 'Some Issues Concerning the Effectiveness of Parallel Strategies in R and D projects', *IEEE Transactions on Engineering Management*, EM-18 (1971) pp. 80–9.
30. See M. Gort, *Diversification and Integration in American Industry* (Princeton, 1962) and P. K. Gorecki, 'An Inter-industry Analysis of Diversification in the UK Manufacturing Sector', *Journal of Industrial Economics* 24 (1975) pp. 131–46.
31. See L. R. Amey, 'Diversified Manufacturing Business', *Journal of the Royal Statistical Society*, Series A, 127 (1964); C. H. Berry, 'Corporate Growth and Diversification', *Journal of Law and Economics* 14 (1971); and P. K. Gorecki, 'The Measurement of Enterprise Diversification', *Review of Economics and Statistics* 56 (1974).
32. See J. F. Weston and S. K. Mansinghka, 'Tests of the Efficiency of Conglomerate Firms', *Journal of Finance* 26 (1971) p. 919.
33. See M. A. Utton, 'Mergers, Diversification and Profit Stability', *Business Ratios* 3 (1969).
34. See Wind, op. cit.; Inso, op. cit.; and E. M. Tauber, 'Why Concept and Product Tests Fail to Predict New Product Results', *Journal of Marketing* 39 (1975) pp. 69–71.
35. For literature on the diffusion process, see the bibliography in Midgley, op. cit.
36. E. M. Rogers, *The Diffusion of Innovations* (New York, 1962).
37. For discussion of this point, see M. Stone, *Product Planning* (London, 1976) Chapter 4.

CHAPTER 9

1. For a recent survey of the literature, see Y. Wind, 'Issues and Advances in Segmentation Research', *Journal of Marketing Research* 15 (1978) pp. 317–37.
2. See R. E. Frank and W. F. Massy, 'Market Segmentation and the Effectiveness of a Brand's Price and Dealing Policies', *Journal of Business* 38 (1965) pp. 186–200, for a conclusion that loyalty may bear no relation to sensitivity to marketing policy.
3. See, for example, J. Bain, *Barriers to New Competition* (Cambridge, Mass. 1956); H. Mann, 'Seller Concentration, Barriers to Entry and Rates of Return in 30 Industries, 1950–1960', *Review of Economics and Statistics* 48 (1966); S. R. Holtermann, 'Market Structure and Economic Performance in UK Manufacturing Industry', *Journal of Industrial Economics* 22 (1973) pp. 119–39; L. E. Preston, *Concentration and Price–Cost Margins in Manufacturing Industries* (Berkeley, Calif., 1968); P. Hart, 'Competition and Rates of Return on Capital in UK Industries', *Business Ratios* 2 (1968); and R. A. Miller, 'Market Structure and Industrial Performance: Relation of Profit Rates to Concentration, Advertising Intensity and Diversity', *Journal of Industrial Economics* 17 (1969) p. 104.
4. See J. S. Bain, 'The Relation of Profit Rate to Industry Concentration in American Manufacturing 1936–40', *Quarterly Journal of Economics* 65 (1951) p. 293 and J. W. Meehan and T. Duchesneau, 'The Critical Level of

Concentration: an Empirical Analysis', *Journal of Industrial Economics* 22 (1974) pp. 21–36.

5. Miller, op. cit.

6. See Holtermann, op. cit., for discussion of this point.

7. For discussion of the impact of foreign firms, see W. G. Shepherd, 'Structure and Behaviour in British Industries, with US Comparisons', *Journal of Industrial Economics* 21 (1972–3) pp. 35–54.

8. See J. H. Dunning, *American Investment in British Industry*, Political and Economic Planning Broadsheet 304 (London, 1969).

9. See S. J. Prais, 'The Growth in Industrial Concentration: a Theoretical Excursus', NIESR Mimeo (London, 1972).

10. See, for example, *Report on the Census of Production 1968* (HMSO, 1974), p. 1158, Table 44, and Shepherd, op. cit.

11. See J. F. Pickering, *Industrial Structure and Market Conduct* (London, 1974) Chapter 4, for a general analysis of barriers to entry.

12. See D. Orr, 'An Index of Entry Barriers and its Application to the Market Structure–Performance Relationship', *Journal of Industrial Economics* 12 (1964) pp. 39–49, for discussion of this point.

13. See Orr, op. cit.

14. See Y. S. Hu, *The Marketing Threshold* (Centre for Business Research, Manchester Business School, Research Report, 1973).

15. See E. T. Penrose, *The Theory of the Growth of the Firm* (Oxford, 1963) Chapter 10, for discussion of this point.

16. See J. Bain, *Industrial Organisation* (New York, 2nd edn, 1968) pp. 218 and 221; Penrose, op. cit., pp. 220–5; and D. Needham, *Economic Analysis and Industrial Structure* (New York, 1969) p. 95, for arguments to this effect.

17. R. Nelson, 'Market Growth, Competition, Diversification and Product Concentration, 1947–1954', *Journal of the American Statistical Association* (1960) pp. 640–9 and W. Shepherd, 'Trends of Concentration in American Manufacturing Industries 1947–58', *Review of Economics and Statistics* 46 (1964) pp. 200–12, support the contention that the level of concentration falls, while D. Kamerschen, 'Market Growth and Industry Concentration', *Journal of the American Statistical Association* (1968) pp. 228–41, does not support it. However, there are problems in the first two studies as a result of the choice of base year and with the third because of the short period of study.

18. See Bain (1968) op. cit., pp. 241–50; R. Caves, *American Industry: Structure, Conduct and Performance* (Englewood Cliffs, N.J., 2nd edn, 1967) 34; and F. M. Scherer, *Industrial Market Structure and Economic Performance* (Chicago, 1970) pp. 129, 130 and 343.

19. For support of this point, see J. A. Dalton and S. A. Rhoades, 'Growth and Product Differentiability as Factors Influencing Changes in Concentration', *Journal of Industrial Economics* 23 (1974) pp. 235–40.

20. This point is also supported by the results of Dalton and Rhoades, op. cit.

21. See E. von Hippel, 'A Customer Active Paradigm for Industrial Product Idea Generation', *Research Policy* 7 (1978) pp. 240–66, for the importance of learning from customers.

22. For further analysis of this point, see The Betro Trust, *Concentration on Key Markets* (London, 1977) and S. Hirsch and B. Lev, 'Sales Stabilisation through Export Diversification', *Review of Economics and Statistics* 53 (1971) pp. 270–9.

CHAPTER 10

1. See A. Gabor and C. W. J. Granger, 'On the Price Consciousness of Consumers', *Applied Statistics* 10 (1961) pp. 170–88; M. T. Cunningham and J. G. Whyte, 'The Behaviour of Industrial Buyers in Their Search for Suppliers of Machine Tools', *Journal of Management Studies* 11 (1974) pp. 115–28; and G. L. Wise and A. L. King, 'Price Awareness in the Gasoline Market', *Journal of Retailing* 49 (1973) pp. 64–76.
2. See R. A. Peterson, 'The Price – Perceived Quality Relationship, the Empirical Evidence', *Journal of Marketing Research* 7 (1970) pp. 525–8; R. S. Mason, 'Price and Product Quality Assessment', *European Journal of Marketing* 8 (1975) pp. 29–41; and A. Gabor and C. W. J. Granger, 'Price as an Indicator of Quality', *Economica* 33 (1966) pp. 43–70.
3. See D. C. Hague, *Pricing in Business* (London, 1971) for a comprehensive analysis of pricing objectives.
4. For evidence on this, see K. Couts, W. Godley and W. D. Nordhaus, *Industrial Pricing in the United Kingdom* (Cambridge, 1978).
5. For the original work on the subject, see P. Sylos-Labini, *Oligopoly and Technical Progress* (Cambridge, Mass., 1962). For further discussion, see M. I. Kamien and N. L. Schwartz, 'Limit Pricing and Uncertain Entry', *Econometrica* 39 (1971) pp. 441–54.
6. For an example of the operation of price leadership policies and the problems associated with them, see R. W. Shaw, 'Price Leadership and the Effect of New Entry in the UK Retail Petrol Supply Market', *Journal of Industrial Economics* 23 (1974) pp. 65–79.
7. Note that this may not be beneficial to the dominant firm. See D. A. Worcester, Jr., 'Why "Dominant Firms" Decline', *Journal of Political Economy* 65 (1957) pp. 338–46.
8. See F. Edelman, 'The Art and Science of Competitive Bidding', *Harvard Business Review*, July–August 1965.
9. For discussion of optimal transfer pricing policies, see J. Hirshleifer, 'On the Economics of Transfer Pricing', *Journal of Business* 29 (1956) p. 172.
10. See J. Dean, 'The Pricing of Pioneer Products', *Journal of Industrial Economics* 17 (1969) pp. 165–79.

CHAPTER 11

1. For discussion of the information-provision aspects, see L. G. Telser, 'Supply and Demand for Advertising Messages', *American Economic Review* 56 (1966) p. 457; P. K. Else, 'The Incidence of Advertising in Manufacturing Industries', *Oxford Economic Papers* 18 (1966) p. 88; and P.

Doyle, 'Advertising Expenditure and Consumer Demand', *Oxford Economic Papers* 20 (1968) p. 394.

2. See N. H. Borden, *The Economic Effects of Advertising* (Homewood, Ill., 1942).
3. For analysis of the relation between advertising and distribution systems, see N. Kaldor, 'The Economic Aspects of Advertising', *Review of Economic Studies* 18 (1950) p. 1.
4. For general analysis of this topic, see M. Alemson, 'Advertising and the Nature of Competition', *Economic Journal* 81 (1970) p. 282 and P. Doyle, 'Economic Aspects of Advertising: a Survey', *Economic Journal* 78 (1968) p. 570.
5. For the original work on this topic, see R. L. Hall and C. J. Hitch, 'Price Theory and Business Behaviour', *Oxford Economic Papers* 2 (1939) p. 12. For a review of work in this area, see A. Silberston, 'The Price Behaviour of Firms', *Economic Journal* 80 (1970) p. 511.
6. See Doyle, 'Economic Aspects'; H. M. Mann, J. A. Heeming and J. W. Meehan, 'Advertising and Concentration, an Empirical Investigation', *Journal of Industrial Economics* 16 (1967) p. 34; L. A. Guth, 'Advertising and Market Structures Revisited', *Journal of Industrial Economics* 19 (1971) p. 179; C. J. Sutton, 'Advertising, Concentration and Competition', *Economic Journal* 84 (1974) pp. 56–69; and L. G. Telser, 'Advertising and Competition', *Journal of Political Economy* 72 (1964) pp. 537–62.
7. See W. S. Comanor and T. A. Wilson, 'Advertising, Market Structure and Performance', *Review of Economics and Statistics* 49 (1967) pp. 423–40; J. M. Vernon and R. M. Nourse, 'Profit Rates and Market Structure of Advertising Intensive Firms', *Journal of Industrial Economics* 22 (1973) pp. 1–20; R. A. Miller, 'Market Structure and Industrial Performance: Relation of Profit Rates to Concentration, Advertising Intensity and Diversity', *Journal of Industrial Economics* 17 (1969) pp. 104–18; and L. W. Weiss, 'Advertising, Profits and Corporate Taxes', *Review of Economics and Statistics* 51 (1969) pp. 421–30.
8. See K. Cowling, J. Cable, M. Kelly and T. McGuiness, *Advertising and Economic Behaviour* (London, 1975) Chapter 7.
9. See O. E. Williamson, 'Selling Expense as a Barrier to Entry', *Quarterly Journal of Economics* 77 (1963).
10. For reviews of the literature, see K. S. Palda, 'Sales Effects of Advertising: A Review of the Literature', *Journal of Advertising Research* 4 (1964) pp. 12–16 and A. G. Rao and P. B. Miller, 'Advertising/Sales Response Functions', *Journal of Advertising Research* 15 (1975) pp. 7–15.
11. See, for example, L. J. Parsons, 'The Product Life Cycle and Time Varying Advertising Elasticities', *Journal of Marketing Research* 12 (1975) pp. 476–80 and A. G. Sawyer, 'The Effects of Repetition of Refutational and Supportive Advertising Appeals', *Journal of Marketing Research* 10 (1973) pp. 23–33.
12. See, for example, T. S. Robertson, 'Purchase Sequence Responses: Innovators vs. Non-innovators', *Journal of Advertising Research* 4 (1968) pp. 47–52.
13. For an example of analysis of promotional mix decisions using an economics-related technique, see J. F. Engel and M. R. Warshaw,

'Allocating Advertising Dollars by Linear Programming', *Journal of Advertising Research* 4 (1964) pp. 42–8.

14. An exception to this is Cowling et al, op. cit., Chapter 3, where the notion of messages transmitted by different media is discussed and its implication for overall advertising cost variables used in most economic studies is considered.

15. See Cowling et al., op. cit., pp. 20–2.

16. The analysis of Cowling et al. proceeds as follows:
If we start with a demand function for the product:

$$Q_t = f(p_t, p_{t-1}, \ldots, \text{etc.}; Y_t, Y_{t-1}, \ldots, \text{etc.}; A_t, A_{t-1}, \ldots, \text{etc.}),$$

where p = price, Y = income of consumer and A = advertising expenditure, then the simple Koyck transformation (assuming linear form and assuming that the effect of each independent variable X is of the form

$$b_X(X_t + gX_{t-1} + g^2 X_{t-2} + \ldots, \text{etc.}),$$

where the g's are the declining weights) is given by

$$Q_t = (1 - g)b_0 + b_p p_t + b_Y Y_t + b_A A_t + gQ_{t-1}$$

where b_0 is the intercept term. The lagged values of advertising A are then introduced again into the transformation with a second set of declining weights. Note that this implies that Q_{t-1} and Q_{t-2} will both appear on the left hand side, possibly posing problems of multicollinearity.

17. See, for example, F. M. Bass, 'A Simultaneous Equation Regression Study of Advertising and the Sales of Cigarettes', *Journal of Marketing Research* 6 (1969).

18. See K. Cowling and J. Cubbin, 'Price, Quality and Advertising Competition: an Econometric Analysis of the UK Car Market', *Economica* 38 (1971); J. J. Lambin, 'Advertising and Competitive Behaviour: A Case Study', *Applied Economics* 2 (1970) p. 231; L. G. Telser, 'Advertising and Cigarettes', *Journal of Political Economy* 70 (1962); and Bass, op. cit.

19. For further discussion of this point, see R. Haveman and G. De Bartolo, 'The Revenue Maximising Oligopoly Model, a Comment', *American Economic Review* 58 (1968).

20. R. Dorfman and P. Steiner, in their 'Optimal Advertising and Optimal Quality', *American Economic Review* 44 (1954) pp. 826–36, produce a general statement of the optimal conditions. The Dorfman – Steiner theorem states that if a single product firm can manipulate price, quality and advertising, it will find itself at the profit maximising point where the numerical value of the price elasticity of demand, the numerical value of the marginal sales effect of advertising and the numerical value of the product of quality elasticity and mark-up over average cost are all equal. For proof of this, see the original article. For a summary of this and related ideas, see W. D. Reekie, *Managerial Economics* (Oxford 1975) Chapter 3.

21. See Cowling et al., op. cit., Chapter 4, for results and discussion.

22. See Cowling and Cubbin, op. cit.

CHAPTER 12

1. For analysis of the 'internal' aspects of distribution systems, see C. Fulop, *Competition for Consumers* (London 1964); R. Cox, *Distribution in a High Level Economy* (Englewood Cliffs, N.J., 1965); L. W. Stern and A. I. El-Ansary, *Marketing Channels* (Englewood Cliffs, N.J., 1977); W. G. McClelland, *Costs and Competition in Retailing* (London, 1967); D. J. Dalrymple and D. L. Thompson, *Retailing: an Economic View* (New York, 1969); and L. P. Bucklin, *A Theory of Distribution Channel Structure* (Berkeley, Calif., 1966).
2. For discussion of the effect of the common carrier on the economics of distribution, see F. J. Beier, 'The Role of the Common Carrier in the Channel of Distribution', *Transportation Journal* 9 (Winter 1969) pp. 12–21.
3. For discussion of channel cost analysis, see M. Zober, *Marketing Management* (New York, 1964) pp. 241 and 267. For discussion of the general issues surrounding the efficiency of distribution systems, see Cox, op. cit., Part III and M. Hall et al., *Distribution in Great Britain and North America: A Study in Structure and Productivity* (London, 1961). See R. Lekashman and J. F. Stolle, 'The Total Cost Approach to Distribution', *Business Horizons* 8 (Winter 1965) pp. 34–46, for discussion of physical distribution aspects.
4. For general analysis of the relationship between promotion and distribution, see B. Shapiro, 'Improve Distribution with Your Promotional Mix', *Harvard Business Review*, March–April 1977, pp. 115–23.
5. The thesis, put forward by J. K. Galbraith in *American Capitalism* (London, 1952) that power produces 'countervailing power' has been challenged by various writers, including A. Hunter in 'Notes on Countervailing Power', *Economic Journal* 68 (1958) pp. 89–103 and J. P. Miller, 'Competition and Countervailing Power', *American Economic Review* 44 (1954) pp. 15–25. The evidence seems to demonstrate that the tendency for countervailing power to be generated is not strong enough to justify general assumptions of Galbraith's kind.
6. For general discussions of bargaining, see J. Harsanyi, 'Measurement of Social Power, Opportunity Costs and the Theory of Two-Person Bargaining Games', *Behavioural Science* 7 (1962) pp. 67–80; R. L. Bishop, 'A Zeuthen–Hicks Theory of Bargaining', *Econometrica* 32 (1964) pp. 410–17; J. G. Cross, 'A Theory of the Bargaining Process', *American Economic Review* 55 (1965) pp. 67–94; L. Foldes, 'A Determinate Model of Bilateral Monopoly', *Economica* 31 (1964) pp. 117–31; A. L. Bowley, 'Bilateral Monopoly', *Economic Journal* 38 (1928) pp. 651–9; W. Fellner, 'Prices and Wages under Bilateral Monopoly', *Quarterly Journal of Economics* 61 (1947) pp. 503–32; and H. H. Baligh and L. E. Richartz, *Vertical Market Structures* (Boston, Mass., 1967).
7. For comprehensive analysis of the determinants of power in distribution channels, see F. J. Beier and L. W. Stern, 'Power in the Channel of Distribution' in L. W. Stern (ed.), *Distribution Channels, Behavioural Dimensions* (Boston, Mass., 1969) pp. 92–116; S. D. Hunt and J. R. Nevin, 'Power in a Channel of Distribution: Sources and Consequences', *Journal of*

Marketing Research 11 (May 1974) pp. 186–93; and A. I. El-Ansary and L. W. Stern, 'Power Measurement in the Distribution Channel', *Journal of Marketing Research* 9 (February 1972) pp. 47–52. For discussion of the vertical integration option, see S. H. Logan, 'A Conceptual Framework for Analysing the Economies of Vertical Integration', *American Journal of Agricultural Economics* 51 (1969) pp. 836–48.

8. This analysis is an extension of that of Harsanyi, op. cit.

9. For discussion of the role of information provision, see J. R. Grabner, Jr. and L. J. Rosenberg, 'Communication in Distribution Channel Systems' in Stern, op. cit. (1969).

10. For discussion of the impact of these factors, see M. E. Porter, 'Consumer Behaviour, Retailer Power and Market Performance in Consumer Goods Industries', *Review of Economics and Statistics* 56 (1974). For discussion of the factors affecting power bases, see R. B. Heflebower, 'Mass Distribution: a Phase of Bilateral Oligopoly or of Competition', *American Economic Review* 47 (1957) pp. 274–85 and B. Mallen, 'Channel Power: A Form of Economic Exploitation', *European Journal of Marketing* 12 (1978) pp. 194–201.

11. For an analysis of the use of postponement of supply or payment to shift risk to the other party, see W. Alderson, 'Marketing Efficiency and the Principle of Postponement', *Cost and Profit Outlook* 3 (1950); L. P. Bucklin, 'Postponement, Speculation and the Structure of Distribution Channels' in his *The Marketing Channel: A Conceptual Viewpoint* (New York, 1967) pp. 67–74 and B. Contini, 'The Value of Time in Bargaining Negotiations: Some Experimental Evidence', *American Economic Review* 58 (1968) pp. 374–93.

12. For analysis of the effects of resale price maintenance, see J. F. Pickering, *Resale Price Maintenance in Practice* (London, 1966).

13. For a discussion of the disadvantages of uncoordinated distribution channels, see B. C. McCammon, Jr., 'Perspectives for Distribution Programming' in L. P. Bucklin (ed.), *Vertical Marketing Systems* (Glenview, Ill., 1970). Note that channel coordination requires inter-organisational decision making, which tends to be substantially more complicated than intra-organisational decision making (see M. Tuite et al. (eds.), *Interorganisational Decision Making* (Chicago, 1972).

14. For examples of this, see McCammon, op. cit.

15. See D. N. Thompson, 'Contractual Marketing Systems: an Overview' in D. N. Thompson (ed.), *Contractual Marketing Systems* (Lexington, Mass., 1971).

16. See W. R. Davidson, 'Changes in Distributive Institutions', in W. G. Moller, Jr., and D. L. Wilemon (eds.), *Marketing Channels: A Systems Viewpoint* (Homewood, Ill., 1971).

17. For analysis of some of these issues, see J. C. Palamountain, *The Politics of Distribution* (Cambridge, Mass., 1955).

18. For some examples of restrictions, see R. O. Werner, 'Marketing and the United States Supreme Court 1965–68', *Journal of Marketing* 33 (January 1969) p. 20.

Suggestions for Further Study

The manager or student interested in taking his study of the marketing/economics interface further has three basic options. One is to take some formal programme of study in a related field (such as industrial or managerial economics). The reader who has access to good library facilities has the option of following up the references in the end-notes. However, assuming that the typical reader operates under a severe time constraint, the most appropriate option is to use a limited number of broad-coverage books.

General empirical material is provided in texts on industrial economics, such as R. Caves, *American Industry: Structure, Conduct and Performance*, 4th edn (Englewood Cliffs, N.J., 1977), and J. F. Pickering, *Industrial Structure and Market Conduct* (London, 1974). General theoretical material is provided in texts on managerial economics, such as (in order of theoretical complexity): J. Simon, *Applied Managerial Economics* (Englewood Cliffs, N.J., 1975) (a highly readable text); J. Bridge and J. C. Dodds, *Managerial Decision Making* (London, 1975); and W. J. Baumol, *Economic Theory and Operations Analysis*, 4th edn (Englewood Cliffs, N.J., 1977).

For a concise summary of managerial theories of business behaviour, see J. R. Wildsmith, *Managerial Theories of the Firm* (London, 1973). Analysis of decisions, production and cost aspects is covered by the texts on managerial economics. International and development economics aspects are dealt with in R. Vernon and L. T. Wells, *The Economic Environment of International Business*, 2nd edn (Englewood Cliffs, N.J., 1976); their *The Manager in the International Economy*, 3rd edn (Englewood Cliffs, N.J., 1976); and B. M. Richman and M. R. Copen, *International Management and Economic Development* (New York, 1972). For an interesting assessment of the implications of developments in the macroeconomy, see F. C. Allvine and F. A. Tarpley, *The New*

State of the Economy (Englewood Cliffs, N.J., 1977).

Economic aspects of consumer behaviour are covered in S. Ward and T. Robertson (eds), *Consumer Behaviour, Theoretical Sources* (Englewood Cliffs, N.J., 1973). Some interesting empirical results are to be found in G. Katona, B. Strumpel and E. Zahn, *Aspirations and Affluence* (New York, 1971). For a general treatment of the subject, see J. F. Niss, *Consumer Economics* (Englewood Cliffs, N.J., 1974).

Innovation aspects are analysed in C. Freeman, *The Economics of Industrial Innovation* (London, 1974) and E. Mansfield, *The Production and Application of New Industrial Technology* (New York, 1977). Product policy is analysed in M. Stone, *Product Planning* (London, 1976). For a recent study of some of the factors influencing market choice, see L. Hannah and J. Kay, *Concentration in Modern Industry* (London, 1977).

On pricing, see F. Livesey, *Pricing* (London, 1976) and J. V. Koch, *Industrial Organisation and Prices* (Englewood Cliffs, N.J., 1974). On promotion, see K. Cowling *et al., Advertising and Economic Behaviour* (London, 1975). For a comprehensive analysis of distribution, see L. W. Stern and A. I. El-Ansary, *Marketing Channels* (Englewood Cliffs, N.J., 1977).

Index